by Stanley Kunitz

INTELLECTUAL THINGS *(poems)*

PASSPORT TO THE WAR *(poems)*

SELECTED POEMS 1928–1958

POEMS OF JOHN KEATS *(editor)*

THE TESTING-TREE *(poems)*

POEMS OF AKHMATOVA *(translator,* with Max Hayward)

STORY UNDER FULL SAIL, by Andrei Voznesensky *(translator)*

THE COAT WITHOUT A SEAM *(poems: limited edition)*

THE TERRIBLE THRESHOLD *(English edition only)*

A KIND OF ORDER, A KIND OF FOLLY: Essays & Conversations

ORCHARD LAMPS, by Ivan Drach *(editor and co-translator)*

THE POEMS OF STANLEY KUNITZ 1928–1978

THE WELLFLEET WHALE AND COMPANION POEMS *(limited edition)*

Next-to-Last Things

Next-to-Last Things

New Poems and Essays by
STANLEY KUNITZ

The Atlantic Monthly Press
BOSTON / NEW YORK

FIRST EDITION

LIBRARY OF CONGRESS CATALOGING-IN-PUBLICATION DATA

Kunitz, Stanley.
  Next-to-last things.

  I. Title.
PS3521.U7N4 1985   811'.52   85-47995
ISBN 0-87113-036-X

Acknowledgments appear on pages 129–130.

MV

Published simultaneously in Canada

PRINTED IN THE UNITED STATES OF AMERICA

And he forsook the last things,
the dear inviolable mysteries —
Plato's lamp, passed from the hand
of saint to saint —
that he might risk his soul in the streets,
where the things given
are only next to last . . .

                          — *Around Pastor Bonhoeffer*

CONTENTS

I

"I will try to speak of the beauty of
shapes, and I do not mean, as most people
would suppose, the shapes of living figures,
or their imitations in painting, but I mean
straight lines and curves and the shapes made
from them by the lathe, ruler or square. They
are not beautiful for any particular reason or
purpose, as other things are, but are eternally,
and by their very nature, beautiful, and give
a pleasure of their own quite free from the
itch of desire. . . ."

— Socrates, in the *Philebus* of Plato

THE SNAKES OF SEPTEMBER

All summer I heard them
rustling in the shrubbery,
outracing me from tier
to tier in my garden,
a whisper among the viburnums,
a signal flashed from the hedgerow,
a shadow pulsing
in the barberry thicket.
Now that the nights are chill
and the annuals spent,
I should have thought them gone,
in a torpor of blood
slipped to the nether world
before the sickle frost.
Not so. In the deceptive balm
of noon, as if defiant of the curse
that spoiled another garden,
these two appear on show
through a narrow slit
in the dense green brocade
of a north-country spruce,
dangling head-down, entwined
in a brazen love-knot.
I put out my hand and stroke
the fine, dry grit of their skins.
After all,
we are partners in this land,
co-signers of a covenant.
At my touch the wild
braid of creation
trembles.

THE ABDUCTION

Some things I do not profess
to understand, perhaps
not wanting to, including
whatever it was they did
with you or you with them
that timeless summer day
when you stumbled out of the wood,
distracted, with your white blouse torn
and a bloodstain on your skirt.
"Do you believe?" you asked.
Between us, through the years,
from bits, from broken clues,
we pieced enough together
to make the story real:
how you encountered on the path
a pack of sleek, grey hounds,
trailed by a dumbshow retinue
in leather shrouds; and how
you were led, through leafy ways,
into the presence of a royal stag,
flaming in his chestnut coat,
who kneeled on a swale of moss
before you; and how you were borne
aloft in triumph through the green,
stretched on his rack of budding horn,
till suddenly you found yourself alone
in a trampled clearing.

That was a long time ago,
almost another age, but even now,
when I hold you in my arms,

I wonder where you are.
Sometimes I wake to hear
the engines of the night thrumming
outside the east bay window
on the lawn spreading to the rose garden.
You lie beside me in elegant repose,
a hint of transport hovering on your lips,
indifferent to the harsh green flares
that swivel through the room,
searchlights controlled by unseen hands.
Out there is childhood country,
bleached faces peering in
with coals for eyes.
Our lives are spinning out
from world to world;
the shapes of things
are shifting in the wind.
What do we know
beyond the rapture and the dread?

RACCOON JOURNAL

July 14
rac-coon', n. from the American Indian (Algonquian)
arahkunem, "he scratches with the hands."
— *New World Dictionary*

July 17

They live promiscuously in the woods
above the marsh, snuggling in hollow trees
or rock-piled hillside dens,
from which they swagger in dead of night,
nosy, precocious, bushy-tailed,
to inspect their properties in town.

At every house they drop a calling card,
doorstep deposits of soft reddish scats
and heavy sprays of territorial scent
that on damp mornings mixes with the dew.

August 21–26

I've seen them, under the streetlight,
paddling up the lane,
five pelts in single file,
halting in unison to topple
a garbage can and gorge
on lobster shells and fish heads
or scattered parts of chicken.

Last year my neighbor's dog,
a full-grown Labrador retriever,
chased a grizzly old codger
into the tidal basin,
where shaggy arms reached up
from the ooze to embrace him,

[6]

dragging his muzzle under
until at length he drowned.

There's nobody left this side
of Gull Hill to tangle
with them, certainly not
my superannuated cat,
domesticated out of nature,
who stretches by the stove
and puts on a show of bristling.
She does that even when mice
go racing round the kitchen.
We seem to be two of a kind,
though that's not to say I'm happy
paying my vegetable tithe
over and over
out of ripe summer's bounty
to feed omnivorous appetites,
or listening to the scratch of prowlers
from the fragrant terraces, as they
dig-dig-dig, because they're mad
for bonemeal, uprooting plants and bulbs,
whole clumps, squirming and dank,
wherever they catch a whiff
of buried angel dust.

October 31

To be like Orpheus, who could talk
with animals in their own language:
in sleep I had that art, but now
I've waked into the separate
wilderness of age,
where the old, libidinous beasts
assume familiar shapes,
pretending to be tamed.

Raccoons! I can hear them
confabulating on the porch,
half-churring, half-growling,

[7]

bubbling to a manic hoot
that curdles the night-air.
Something out there appalls.
On the back door screen
a heavy furpiece hangs,
spreadeagled, breathing hard,
hooked by prehensile fingers,
with its pointed snout pressing in,
and the dark agates of its bandit eyes
furiously blazing. Behind,
where shadows deepen, burly forms
lumber from side to side
like diminished bears
in a flatfooted shuffle.
They watch me, unafraid.
I know they'll never leave,
they've come to take possession.

Provincetown 1984

THE TUMBLING OF WORMS

Back in the thirties, in the midst of the Depression, I fled the city and moved to a Connecticut farm. It was the period of my first marriage. We lived in an old gambrel house, built about 1740, on top of a ridge called Wormwood Hill. I had bought the house, together with more than 100 acres of woodland and pasture, for $500 down. It had no electricity, no heat, no running water, and it was in bad repair, but it was a great, beautiful house. I spent most of three years, working with my hands, making it habitable. At that time early American art and furniture were practically being given away. Poor as we were, we managed to fill the house with priceless stuff. We were so far from the city and from all signs of progress that we might as well have been living in another age.

One spring there appeared on the road, climbing up the hill, a man in a patchwork suit, with a battered silk hat on his head. His trousers and swallow-tail coat had been mended so many times, with varicolored swatches, that when he approached us, over the brow of the hill, he looked like a crazy-quilt on stilts.

He was an itinerant tinker, dried-out and old, thin as a scarecrow, with a high, cracked voice. He asked for pots and pans to repair, scissors and knives to sharpen. In the shade of the sugar maples, that a colonel in Washington's army was said to have planted, he set up his shop and silently went to work on the articles I handed to him.

When he was done, I offered him lunch in the kitchen. He would not sit down to eat, but accepted some food in a bag. "I have been here before," he said to me quietly. On our way out, while we were standing in the front hall at the foot of the staircase, he suddenly cried, "I hear the worms tumbling in this house." "What do you mean?" I asked. He did not answer, but cupped his hands over his eyes. I took it as a bad omen, a fateful prophecy, about my house, my marriage. And so it turned out to be.

Some time later I learned that my visitor was a legendary figure, known throughout the countryside as the Old Darned Man. He had been a brilliant divinity student at Yale, engaged to a childhood sweetheart, with the wedding set for the day after graduation. But on that very day, while he waited at the church, the news was brought to him that she had run off with his dearest friend. Ever since then he had been wandering distractedly from village to village in his wedding clothes.

As for the worms, they belonged to a forgotten page in local history. Late in the nineteenth century the housewives of the region, dreaming of a fortune to be made, had started a cottage industry in silkworm culture, importing the worms from China. The parlors of every farmhouse were lined with stacks of silkworm trays, in which the worms munched on mulberry leaves, making clicking and whispering noises. That was the sound heard in my hall.

It's a story without a happy ending. The worms died; the dreams of riches faded; abandoned plows rusted in the farmyards; one breathless summer day a black-funneled twister wheeled up Wormwood Hill from the stricken valley, dismantling my house, my barn, my grove of sugar maples; the face of my bride darkened and broke into a wild laughter; I never saw the Old Darned Man again.

THE SCENE

— after Alexander Blok

Night. Street. Lamp. Drugstore.
A world of dim and sleazy light.
You may live twenty-five years more.
Nothing will change. No way out.

You die. You're born again and all
Will be repeated as before:
The cold ripple of a canal.
Night. Street. Lamp. Drugstore.

THE IMAGE-MAKER

A wind passed over my mind,
insidious and cold.
It is a thought, I thought,
but it was only its shadow.
Words came,
or the breath of my sisters,
with a black rustle of wings.
They came with a summons
that followed a blessing.
I could not believe
I too would be punished.
Perhaps it is time to go,
to slip alone, as at a birth,
out of this glowing house
where all my children danced.
Seductive Night! I have stood
at my casement the longest hour,
watching the acid wafer
of the moon slowly dissolving
in a scud of cloud, and heard
the farthest hidden stars
calling my name.
I listen, but I avert my ears
from Meister Eckhart's warning:
All things must be forsaken.
God scorns
to show Himself among images.

LAMPLIGHTER: 1914

What I remember most was not
the incident at Sarajevo,
but the first flying steamkettle
puffing round the bend,
churning up the dirt
between the rocky pastures
as it came riding high
on its red wheels
in a blare of shining brass;
and my bay stallion snorting,
rearing in fright, bolting,
leaving me sprawled on the ground;
and our buggy
careening out of sight,
those loose reins dangling,
racing toward its rendezvous
with Hammond's stone wall
in an explosion of wood and flesh,
the crack of smashed cannon bones.
Who are these strangers
sprung out of the fields?
It is my friend, almost my brother,
who points a gun
to the crooked head.

Once I was a lamplighter
on the Quinnapoxet roads,
making the rounds with Prince,
who was older than I and knew
by heart each of our stations,
needing no whoa of command

nor a tug at his bridle.
That was the summer I practiced
sleight-of-hand and fell asleep
over my picture-books of magic.
Toward dusk, at crossings
and at farmhouse gates,
under the solitary iron trees
I stood on the rim of the buggy wheel
and raised my enchanter's wand,
with its tip of orange flame,
to the gas mantles in their cages,
touching them, one by one,
till the whole countryside bloomed.

DAY OF FOREBODING

Great events are about to happen.
I have seen migratory birds
in unprecedented numbers
descend on the coastal plain,
picking the margins clean.
My bones are a family in their tent
huddled over a small fire
waiting for the uncertain signal
to resume the long march.

THREE SMALL PARABLES FOR MY POET FRIENDS

1

Certain saurian species, notably the skink, are capable of shedding their tails in self-defence when threatened. The detached appendage diverts attention to itself by taking on a life of its own and thrashing furiously about. As soon as the stalking wildcat pounces on the wriggler, snatching it up from the sand to bite and maul it, the free lizard scampers off. A new tail begins to grow in place of the one that has been sacrificed.

2

The larva of the tortoise beetle has the neat habit of collecting its droppings and exfoliated skin into a little packet that it carries over its back when it is out in the open. If it were not for this fecal shield, it would lie naked before its enemies.

3

Among the Bedouins, the beggar poets of the desert are held in contempt because of their greed, their thievery and venality. Everyone in the scattered encampments knows that poems of praise can be bought, even by the worst of scoundrels, for food or money. Furthermore, these wandering minstrels are notorious for stealing the ideas, lines, and even whole songs of others. Often the recitation is interrupted by the shouts of the squatters around the campfire: "Thou liest. Thou stolest it from So-and-so!" When the poet tries to defend himself, calling for witnesses to vouch for his probity or, in extremity, appealing to Allah, his hearers hoot him down, crying, "Kassad, kaddab! A poet is a liar."

THE ROUND

Light splashed this morning
on the shell-pink anemones
swaying on their tall stems;
down blue-spiked veronica
light flowed in rivulets
over the humps of the honeybees;
this morning I saw light kiss
the silk of the roses
in their second flowering,
my late bloomers
flushed with their brandy.
A curious gladness shook me.

So I have shut the doors of my house,
so I have trudged downstairs to my cell,
so I am sitting in semi-dark
hunched over my desk
with nothing for a view
to tempt me
but a bloated compost heap,
steamy old stinkpile,
under my window;
and I pick my notebook up
and I start to read aloud
the still-wet words I scribbled
on the blotted page:
"Light splashed . . ."

I can scarcely wait till tomorrow
when a new life begins for me,
as it does each day,
as it does each day.

PASSING THROUGH

— *on my seventy-ninth birthday*

Nobody in the widow's household
ever celebrated anniversaries.
In the secrecy of my room
I would not admit I cared
that my friends were given parties.
Before I left town for school
my birthday went up in smoke
in a fire at City Hall that gutted
the Department of Vital Statistics.
If it weren't for a census report
of a five-year-old White Male
sharing my mother's address
at the Green Street tenement in Worcester
I'd have no documentary proof
that I exist. You are the first,
my dear, to bully me
into these festive occasions.

Sometimes, you say, I wear
an abstracted look that drives you
up the wall, as though it signified
distress or disaffection.
Don't take it so to heart.
Maybe I enjoy not-being as much
as being who I am. Maybe
it's time for me to practice
growing old. The way I look
at it, I'm passing through a phase:
gradually I'm changing to a word.
Whatever you choose to claim
of me is always yours;
nothing is truly mine
except my name. I only
borrowed this dust.

THE LONG BOAT

When his boat snapped loose
from its moorings, under
the screaking of the gulls,
he tried at first to wave
to his dear ones on shore,
but in the rolling fog
they had already lost their faces.
Too tired even to choose
between jumping and calling,
somehow he felt absolved and free
of his burdens, those mottoes
stamped on his name-tag:
conscience, ambition, and all
that caring.
He was content to lie down
with the family ghosts
in the slop of his cradle,
buffeted by the storm,
endlessly drifting.
Peace! Peace!
To be rocked by the Infinite!
As if it didn't matter
which way was home;
as if he didn't know
he loved the earth so much
he wanted to stay forever.

THE WELLFLEET WHALE

A few summers ago, on Cape Cod, a whale foundered on the beach, a sixty-three-foot finback whale. When the tide went out, I approached him. He was lying there, in monstrous desolation, making the most terrifying noises — rumbling — groaning. I put my hands on his flanks and I could feel the life inside him. And while I was standing there, suddenly he opened his eye. It was a big, red, cold eye, and it was staring directly at me. A shudder of recognition passed between us. Then the eye closed forever. I've been thinking about whales ever since.

— *Journal entry*

I

You have your language too,
     an eerie medley of clicks
          and hoots and trills,
location-notes and love calls,
     whistles and grunts. Occasionally,
          it's like furniture being smashed,
or the creaking of a mossy door,
     sounds that all melt into a liquid
          song with endless variations,
as if to compensate
     for the vast loneliness of the sea.
          Sometimes a disembodied voice
breaks in, as if from distant reefs,
     and it's as much as one can bear
          to listen to its long mournful cry,
a sorrow without name, both more

and less than human. It drags
    across the ear like a record
running down.

2

No wind. No waves. No clouds.
    Only the whisper of the tide,
        as it withdrew, stroking the shore,
a lazy drift of gulls overhead,
    and tiny points of light
        bubbling in the channel.
It was the tag-end of summer.
    From the harbor's mouth
        you coasted into sight,
flashing news of your advent,
    the crescent of your dorsal fin
        clipping the diamonded surface.
We cheered at the sign of your greatness
    when the black barrel of your head
        erupted, ramming the water,
and you flowered for us
    in the jet of your spouting.

3

All afternoon you swam
    tirelessly round the bay,
        with such an easy motion,
the slightest downbeat of your tail,
    an almost imperceptible
        undulation of your flippers,
you seemed like something poured,
    not driven; you seemed
        to marry grace with power.
And when you bounded into air,
    slapping your flukes,
        we thrilled to look upon
pure energy incarnate
    as nobility of form.
        You seemed to ask of us

[21]

not sympathy, or love,
   or understanding,
      but awe and wonder.

That night we watched you
   swimming in the moon.
      Your back was molten silver.
We guessed your silent passage
   by the phosphorescence in your wake.
      At dawn we found you stranded on the rocks.

4

There came a boy and a man
   and yet other men running, and two
      schoolgirls in yellow halters
and a housewife bedecked
   with curlers, and whole families in beach
      buggies with assorted yelping dogs.
The tide was almost out.
   We could walk around you,
      as you heaved deeper into the shoal,
crushed by your own weight,
   collapsing into yourself,
      your flippers and your flukes
quivering, your blowhole
   spasmodically bubbling, roaring.
      In the pit of your gaping mouth
you bared your fringework of baleen,
   a thicket of horned bristles.
      When the Curator of Mammals
arrived from Boston
   to take samples of your blood
      you were already oozing from below.
Somebody had carved his initials
   in your flank. Hunters of souvenirs
      had peeled off strips of your skin,
a membrane thin as paper.
   You were blistered and cracked by the sun.

The gulls had been pecking at you.
The sound you made was a hoarse and fitful bleating.

What drew us, like a magnet, to your dying?
    You made a bond between us,
        the keepers of the nightfall watch,
who gathered in a ring around you,
    boozing in the bonfire light.
        Toward dawn we shared with you
your hour of desolation,
    the huge lingering passion
        of your unearthly outcry,
as you swung your blind head
    toward us and laboriously opened
        a bloodshot, glistening eye,
in which we swam with terror and recognition.

5

Voyager, chief of the pelagic world,
    you brought with you the myth
        of another country, dimly remembered,
where flying reptiles
    lumbered over the steaming marshes
        and trumpeting thunder lizards
wallowed in the reeds.
    While empires rose and fell on land,
        your nation breasted the open main,
rocked in the consoling rhythm
    of the tides. Which ancestor first plunged
        head-down through zones of colored twilight
to scour the bottom of the dark?
    You ranged the North Atlantic track
        from Port-of-Spain to Baffin Bay,
edging between the ice-floes
    through the fat of summer,
        lob-tailing, breaching, sounding,
grazing in the pastures of the sea

on krill-rich orange plankton
   crackling with life.
You prowled down the continental shelf,
   guided by the sun and stars
      and the taste of alluvial silt
on your way southward
   to the warm lagoons,
      the tropic of desire,
where the lovers lie belly to belly
   in the rub and nuzzle of their sporting;
      and you turned, like a god in exile,
out of your wide primeval element,
   delivered to the mercy of time.
      Master of the whale-roads,
let the white wings of the gulls
   spread out their cover.
      You have become like us,
disgraced and mortal.

II

1. Grandeur of ideas is founded on precision of ideas.
2. To generalize is to be an idiot. To particularize
   is the alone distinction of merit.
3. He who would do good to another
   must do it in Minute Particulars:
   General Good is the plea of the
   scoundrel, hypocrite & flatterer,
   For Art & Science cannot exist but in minutely
   organized Particulars.

— William Blake, *Jerusalem*

FROM FEATHERS TO IRON

On Thursday, February 19, 1818, John Keats, incited by "the beauty of the morning operating on a sense of idleness," interrupted his revision of Book III of *Endymion* to compose an ebullient letter to his friend John Hamilton Reynolds. "My dear Reynolds," he wrote,

> I had an idea that a Man might pass a very pleasant life in this manner — let him on a certain day read a certain Page of full Poesy or distilled Prose, and let him wander with it, and muse upon it, and reflect upon it, . . . until it becomes stale — but when will it do so? Never. When Man has arrived at a certain ripeness in intellect any one grand and spiritual passage serves him as a starting-post towards all "the two-and-thirty Palaces." How happy is such a voyage of conception, what delicious diligent Indolence!

Keats was then twenty-two. Those two-and-thirty Palaces were the thirty-two "places of delight" in the Buddhist doctrine, of which he had a smattering of knowledge. He was full of curiosity and he was fascinated by the play of the mind, which evoked for him the image of the spider unreeling gossamer from her belly, with no need for more than a few contact points, some convenient leaves and twigs, on which to hang her "airy Citadel." I am correcting Keats here, with respect to gender, for apparently he was unaware that the male spider has no gift or time for spinning, busy as he is with his fatal occupation of roving lecher.

Less than a month later, on Friday, March 13, from his temporary quarters in Devonshire, where he had gone for rest and relaxation, Keats pursued his investigation of the operations of the mind in a letter to Benjamin Bailey. "Every point of thought is the centre of an intellectual world — the two uppermost thoughts in a Man's mind are the two poles of his World," he wrote; "he revolves on them and every thing is southward or northward to him through their means. We take but three steps from feathers to iron."

Ever since I came across that passage in my youth, when I was about the same age as Keats, I have carried it in my head as a glowing touchstone, and walked around it, at first quite cautiously, and examined it, and tried to fathom its cryptic radiations. Among the things it says to me is that no two minds are the same; that each mind is a self-contained universe turning on its obsessional axis; and that at the same time it is a field of dialectical energy charged by what it most affirms and most denies. I am reminded of the paradox presented early in the century by the presumption of the existence of waves of matter on the one hand and particles of light on the other. Which was the correct picture? The German physicists Heisenberg and Born solved the dilemma by asserting that both pictures were equally true. From then on, official sanction having been given, it became possible to describe quantum phenomena whichever way one chose, according to the demands of the occasion. It took but three steps from waves to particles.

I can think of nothing more miraculous than the power of the mind to transform, to connect, to communicate. Some years ago, in a state of unusual agitation, I wrote a poem that owes some of its feeling and substance to the aforementioned passage from Keats, though nobody, as far as I know, has ever detected the relationship. "Green Ways" is its title.

> Let me not say it, let me not reveal
> How like a god my heart begins to climb
> The trellis of the crystal
> In the rose-green moon;
> Let me not say it, let me leave untold
> This legend, while the nights snow emerald.
>
> Let me not say it, let me not confess
> How in the leaflight of my green-celled world

In self's pre-history
The blind moulds kiss;
Let me not say it, let me but endure
This ritual like feather and like star.

Let me proclaim it — human be my lot! —
How from my pit of green horse-bones
I turn, in a wilderness of sweat,
To the moon-breasted sibylline,
And lift this garland, Danger, from her throat
To blaze it in the foundries of the night.

remember feeling at the time, in a kind of transport, that it was
ot I writing the poem, but my cells, my corpuscles, translating
to language the chemistry of a passion. Not until the word *feather*
nnounced itself with absolute assurance of its welcome was I even
aintly aware that Keats had somehow intruded himself into the
rocess of the poem along with Fanny Brawne and my own life
nd love. A student of psychology might legitimately inquire why,
f this explanation is true, Feather did not come to me as one of a
air, companioned by its given antithesis, Iron. It occurs to me —
omething I had never perceived before — that this is exactly what
appened. In the final metaphor, of "the foundries of the night,"
ron makes its obligatory appearance.

No doubt I should credit William Blake with an assist for the
main ingredients of the last line, but my debt to him is fairly ob-
ious and has been many times acknowledged. On the other hand,
vho but myself could know that my readings in the morphology
f fungi and the history of the Irish potato famine of 1845–46 trig-
ered some of the imagery? Poetry, by its nature, is a ganglion of
memories, impressions, influences. A poem without secrets lies dead
n the page. Words themselves come to us dragging their roots
ehind them: roots that are as long as the history of language.

One of my convictions is that at the center of every poetic
magination is a cluster of key images that go back to the poet's
hildhood and that are usually associated with pivotal experiences,
ot necessarily traumatic. Poets are always revisiting the state of
heir innocence, as if to be renewed by it. Carl Jung has observed

[29]

that "no one can free himself from his childhood without firs generously occupying himself with it," but my own feeling is tha the object is not so much to cut oneself off from one's past as t learn how to live with the child you were. That cluster of key im ages is the purest concentration of the self, the individuating node the place where the persona starts. When fresh thoughts and sen sations enter the mind, some of them are drawn into the gravita tional field of the old life and cohere to it. Out of these combinin elements, the more resistant the better, poetry happens. It is idl to weigh the intrinsic worth of the ingredients, for the special min makes something special out of anything. In Keats's case, one ca learn more about his quiddity by pursuing his images of fever an of ooze than by analyzing his literary sources.

A critical property of key images is that they are unalterable being good for a lifetime. Although "the two uppermost thought [as opposed to images] in a Man's mind" may be somewhat les constant, given the factor of a maturing intellect, they are not likel to be unconscionably fickle in a mind of persistent character. In letter to Bailey in the fall of 1817 Keats had written, "I am certai of nothing but of the holiness of the Heart's affections and the trut of Imagination," and he never, in his cruelly brief span, wavere from that axis. Modern writers tend to shy away from such asser tions of principle, but I should find it difficult to separate my ide of D. H. Lawrence from his ideas about Blood and Nature, o Yeats from his fidelity to custom and ceremony, or Eliot from hi theories about the decay of civilization and the need for authority As for myself, I once wrote:

> The manifold tissue of experience, in Whitehead's phrase, with which one is concerned presents itself with a bewildering density, an overlay of episodes and images, both public and private. What makes art possible is that one is also, at the same time, a bundle of simplicities. But modern criticism is frightened of these simplicities. The hard and inescapable phenomenon to be faced is that we are living and dying at once. My commitment is to report the dialogue.

[30]

There is no way of discussing such matters without turning to Coleridge, who laid the cornerstone for our whole structure of thinking about the imagination. The imagination, he said in a celebrated paragraph of *Biographia Literaria,*

> . . . reveals itself in the balance or reconciliation of opposite or discordant qualities: of sameness, with difference; of the general, with the concrete; the idea, with the image; the individual, with the representative; the sense of novelty and freshness, with old and familiar objects; a more than usual state of emotion, with more than usual order. . . .

No one has better described the creative tension that produces a work of art and charges it with energy. Out of our contradictions we build our harmonies. The loom of art requires more than one set of threads: it is the cross-stitching that holds the fabric together. As Blake remarked before Coleridge, "Without Contraries is no progression. Attraction and Repulsion, Reason and Energy, Love and Hate, are necessary to Human existence." He praised the contrary mind, condemned the negative one. We are still learning that the child of negation and denial will be stillborn.

Ultimately poetry does not affect us by meeting any arbitrary tests of metrical or prosodic excellence but by satisfying our hunger for a language that crystallizes our intuitions and makes a syntax out of the crises of our survival. "Man can embody truth," wrote Yeats, "but he cannot know it." It seems to me that the truths of poetry are beyond knowledge. The fallacy is in thinking of the poem as a vessel into which experience is poured or as a skin that serves as cover to a skeleton. On the contrary, the language of poetry is ideally a body-language, inseparable from its maker's breath and living tissue. Every language of civilization has a codified vocabulary and grammar, but poetry, which traces its lineage back to song and dance, and which has never forgotten its origins, is the language of languages.

Here again Coleridge was prescient, anticipating those in our time who entertain the delusion that they have invented the concept of organic form. "The true ground of the mistake," he said with singular clarity in one of his lectures on Shakespeare,

> lies in the confounding mechanical regularity with organic form. The form is mechanic, when on any given material we impress a predetermined form, not necessarily arising out of the properties of the material; — as when to a mass of wet clay we give whatever shape we wish it to retain when hardened. The organic form, on the other hand, is innate; it shapes, as it develops, itself from within, and the fulness of its development is one and the same with the perfection of its outward form.

Unfortunately, in the industrial nexus, it is mechanistic form that imposes itself on our factories and cities, that puts its stamp on our war machines, that strips the earth for the sake of its mineral treasures and deploys regiments of bulldozers across the rolling land to cut straight highways. Walt Whitman's dreams for the American future were sometimes tainted by a burgeoning sense of Manifest Destiny, but he knew what it was that he responded to in the world around him:

> You objects that call from diffusion my meanings and give
>   them shape!
> You light that wraps me and all things in delicate equable
>   showers!
> You paths worn in the irregular hollows by the roadsides!
> I believe you are latent with unseen existences. . . .

Poets are to be trusted only when they are thinking through their senses. Otherwise they are no more trustworthy than anybody else. Their poetry, it should be noted, is more than a form of writing, which is a comparatively late invention of the human species, not much older than Homer, who lived about three thousand years ago. Millions of years before people began to tell about themselves on papyrus and paper, they were accumulating the wisdom of the body,* a cabalistic lore, which not all the books of mankind, now or to come, will ever completely interpret. Sometimes

*For fuller discussion, see essay "The Wisdom of the Body," page 50.

poets travel far and bring back to us news of that other age, re-
membered in our blood, like embers of a sacred fire. I think that
Keats was of that company when, one Sunday in September 1819,
he wrote "To Autumn," the last of the odes, unique in its music
and its majesty.

TO AUTUMN

I

Season of mists and mellow fruitfulness,
   Close bosom-friend of the maturing sun;
Conspiring with him how to load and bless
   With fruit the vines that round the thatch-eaves run;
To bend with apples the moss'd cottage-trees,
   And fill all fruit with ripeness to the core;
     To swell the gourd, and plump the hazel shells
   With a sweet kernel; to set budding more,
And still more, later flowers for the bees,
Until they think warm days will never cease,
     For Summer has o'er-brimm'd their clammy cells.

II

Who hath not seen thee oft amid thy store?
   Sometimes whoever seeks abroad may find
Thee sitting careless on a granary floor,
   Thy hair soft-lifted by the winnowing wind;
Or on a half-reap'd furrow sound asleep,
   Drows'd with the fume of poppies, while thy hook
     Spares the next swath and all its twined flowers:
And sometimes like a gleaner thou dost keep
   Steady thy laden head across a brook;
   Or by a cyder-press, with patient look,
     Thou watchest the last oozings hours by hours.

III

Where are the songs of Spring? Ay, where are they?
   Think not of them, thou hast thy music too, —
While barred clouds bloom the soft-dying day,
   And touch the stubble-plains with rosy hue;
     Then in a wailful choir the small gnats mourn
     Among the river sallows, borne aloft

Or sinking as the light wind lives or dies;
And full-grown lambs loud bleat from hilly bourn;
Hedge-crickets sing; and now with treble soft
The red-breast whistles from a garden-croft;
And gathering swallows twitter in the skies.

And Shakespeare was of that company in the furious com-
bustion of *King Lear*. And, surely, the rhythms of Gerard Manley
Hopkins were body-sprung. Your own body knows it in the lift
and wrenching, the racing and responsive pulse, of his lines, as in
"The Windhover," the poem he thought his best and which he
therefore dedicated "To Christ our Lord":

I caught this morning morning's minion, king-
    dom of daylight's dauphin, dapple-dawn-drawn Falcon, in
    his riding
Of the rolling level underneath him steady air, and striding
High there, how he rung upon the rein of a wimpling wing
In his ecstasy! then off, off forth on swing,
    As a skate's heel sweeps smooth on a bow-bend: the hurl
    and gliding
Rebuffed the big wind. My heart in hiding
Stirred for a bird, — the achieve of, the mastery of the thing!

Keats's famous cry, "O for a Life of Sensations rather than of
Thoughts!," which has been mocked by some and condoned by
others, assumes a new significance if we regard it in the context
of the wisdom of the body. One of the gifts of that wisdom is the
insight that in the chemistry of life the process of catabolism, the
breaking down of our cells, is as essential as its anabolic counter-
part. As a physician by training, Keats was fully aware of the
meaning of his fevers and hemorrhages. His imagination, unable
to reject the dreadful fact of his mortality, ended by embracing it.
Toward the last he wrote, "Verse, Fame, and Beauty are intense
indeed, / But Death intenser." In Taoist doctrine we are told that
division is the same as creation, creation is the same as destruc-
tion, the very lesson that Bakunin taught as the prologue to his
anarchistic revolution and that Dada made programmatic for

Western art. Some of the finest art of the century incorporates certain aspects of that principle.

"When you begin a picture," said Picasso,

> you often make some pretty discoveries. You must be on guard against these. Destroy the thing, do it over several times. In each destroying of a beautiful discovery, the artist does not really suppress it, but rather transforms it, condenses it, makes it more substantial. What comes out in the end is the result of discarded finds. Otherwise, you become your own connoisseur. I sell myself nothing!

Yeats concluded his poignant and yet triumphant poem "The Circus Animals' Desertion," in which he sums up the story of the life of the imagination, with lines that by now must have entered into the consciousness of every living poet:

> Those masterful images because complete
> Grew in pure mind, but out of what began?
> A mound of refuse or the sweepings of a street,
> Old kettles, old bottles, and a broken can,
> Old iron, old bones, old rags, that raving slut
> Who keeps the till. Now that my ladder's gone,
> I must lie down where all the ladders start,
> In the foul rag-and-bone shop of the heart.

Poets, it should be noted, keep shaping their metaphors out of the ruins of their existence, in contradistinction to the powerful on this earth, whose stock-in-trade is the fable of their victories.

In one of his most brilliant perceptions Henri Bergson saw time as resistance — resistance against everything happening at once. Comparably the poet sees himself as an embodiment of resistance — resistance against universal apathy, mediocrity, conformity, against institutional pressures to make everything look and become alike. That is why he is so involved with contraries. Long live the differences! He is not, as some would have it, preparing to settle down in Chaos, where everything *does* happen at once, for he knows too well that though Chaos is an exciting place to visit, he wouldn't want to live there. Cosmos is his other address but the boredom soon sends him packing. What his heart reall desires is neither Chaos nor Cosmos, but Mythos — a new order ing of creation.

He is not content with things as they are. How could he be who has once visited Paradise and kept that vision alive? If it wer not for his dream of perfection, which is the emblem of his life enhancing art, and which he longs to share with others, genera tions of men and women would gradually sink into passivity, ac cepting as their lot second-rate or third-rate destinies, or worse. I one is to be taught submission, in the name of progress or na tional security, it is redemptive to recall the pride of one wh averred that his only humility was toward "the eternal Being, th Principle of Beauty, and the Memory of great Men."

I have never agreed with the sentiment expressed by Auden i his eulogy for Yeats that "poetry makes nothing happen." No doub "Ireland has her madness and her weather still," but Ireland als has the memory of Yeats. His poems have departed from the pag and become places in a spiritual landscape. Here at home poets tol the ghastly truth about Vietnam long before the public had ear for it. Indeed, future chroniclers may record that the turning-point the reversal, in the history of President Johnson's administratio and in the drama of our nation's commitment to the war occurre on June 14, 1965, when poets and artists converted the White Hous Arts Festival into a passionate fiasco. I am happy to confess I playe a role in the planning of that episode.

We poets are citizens too, and most of us have never seen a ivory tower. Of course, we appreciate the unparalleled freedon we enjoy to write as we please. Thank you, Founding Fathers! A the same time we cannot help regretting that only the blessed youn and a handful of incorrigible elders seem to be paying much atten tion to what our poems are saying. Will that be enough to chang the climate of an age?

"I am the truth," said Wallace Stevens, "since I am part of wha is real, but neither more nor less than those around me. And I an

[36]

imagination, in a leaden time and in a world that does not move for the weight of its own heaviness."

The trouble with the old order, as it approaches the twenty-first century, is that it lacks imagination. It fears imagination as it fears truth, for both of them threaten power, contribute to its unease. To stay in office, power must pretend to dignity and honor and compassion, or, failing these, to good fellowship. In its self-satisfaction it does not know it is pretending, for only imagination, which opens the doors of perception to other hearts and minds, is capable of summoning up, in Abraham Lincoln's phrase, "the better angels of our nature."

Consider the words that Lincoln spoke on April 11, 1865, in his last public statement, at the close of a bloody and terrible war, when he faced the necessity of declaring his policy for the reconstruction of the Union. He said:

> We all agree that the seceded states, so called, are out of their proper, practical relation with the Union; and that the sole object of the government, civil and military, in regard to those states is to again get them into that proper practical relation. I believe it is not only possible, but in fact, easier to do this, without deciding or even considering, whether these states have ever been out of the Union, than with it. Finding themselves safely at home, it would be utterly immaterial whether they had ever been abroad. Let us all join in doing the acts necessary to restoring the proper practical relations between these states and the Union; and each forever after, innocently indulge his own opinion whether, in doing the acts, he brought the states from without, into the Union, or only gave them proper assistance, they never having been out of it.

In that magnanimous valedictory, delivered four days before his death, one perceives the beauty of a mind that gives sanction to the hope for amnesty and peace by greeting them and embracing them without a quibble. The poetic imagination, in government as well as in literature, does not ignore or suppress contradictions, but instead seizes the opportunity to create out of them new accommodations, new reconciliations, and new values. It was no accident that the President whom most Americans deem greatest was at once eloquent and compassionate, a man of imagination.

In these days of confusion and alarm, when we yearn for greatness again, it is appropriate to recall Keats's Shakespeare-echoing prayer: "O for a Muse of fire to ascend!"

ROBERT LOWELL: THE SENSE OF A LIFE

I

On the afternoon of Tuesday, September 13, 1977, I was in Naples, in the flag-draped auditorium of the U.S. Information Center, meeting with a small group of university professors to talk with them about American poetry. Our informal conversation had scarcely begun when one of them leaned forward and said, "Have you heard about Mr. Lo-vell? He's dead. Did you know him?" I caught my breath. Did I know him! Yes, in a hundred phases, the myriad contradictions of one who was both Puritan and satyr, alternately silly and wise, modest and arrogant, tender and mean, generous and indifferent, masterful and helpless, depressed and manic.

Everywhere Cal went he brought his turmoil with him, hand in hand with his batch of stained and crumpled manuscripts. "I am tired," he had written. "Everyone is tired of my turmoil." His blue-grey eyes behind his glasses were vague and restless, till they began to glitter. He seemed so full of self, so disconnected from his surroundings, that you could not believe he noticed anything; but somehow, indoors or out, little escaped him. On his next visit to your place he would inquire about a painting or a piece of bric-a-brac that had been moved, joke about the gain in weight of your fat cat Celia, or comment on the most trivial household acquisition. In the garden or on a country walk he would ply you with questions about the names and properties of flowers, about which he appeared to be totally ignorant; but then he would astonish you by publishing a poem that incorporated precise horticultural detail.

His talk was expressive with gesture, the stirring of an invisible broth, interspersed with the shaping of a vase in air — or was it Lilith's archetypal curves that he was fashioning? When he slumped onto your sofa like an extended question mark, tumbler in hand, chain-smoking, dropping his ashes, spouting gossip or poetry, you knew that the moon would have to drift across the sky before he would be ready to go, leaving behind him at least one memorial cigarette hole burnt into cushion or rug. You were bleary with fatigue, but you cherished the rare electricity of his presence. And you would have been desolate if he had not returned.

How could I say all or anything of that to my amiable Italian professors? To them Robert Lowell was an abstract eminence, already historical, a spirit of civilization wafted from on high over the airwaves. *The famous American poet died last night in New York.* No doubt the same report had been flashed to Rome, Paris, Berlin, Madrid, Moscow, Istanbul, and beyond. After Eliot and Pound, had the death of any other American poet been treated as world news? I picked up *The Norton Anthology* that I had brought along with me and read "For the Union Dead" in tribute. What would a foreign audience make of its complex and highly allusive text? Their impression, I soon learned, was that the poem was somehow tied to the Vietnam War, though in truth it had been written several years before we got into that mess. Its density of local Boston color and Civil War documentation was difficult for them to penetrate; yet they listened with polite and even reverential attention. Indeed, fame has its mysteries and advantages.

I have never known anyone so singularly immersed in the career of writing as was Cal. Berryman and Roethke may have vied with him in this respect, but his concentration on the literary landscape was more unremitting: he watched its weather with the diligent attention of a meteorologist, studying its prevailing winds, regularly charting its high and low pressure areas. "All my friends are writers." With his tidy inheritance he had more leisure and fewer responsibilities than most of us. Protected by his physical awkwardness, which did not prevent him on occasion from projecting an image of noble public grace, he avoided being handy around the house; no sports or hobbies distracted him except, perhaps, for the game of rating his contemporaries — the game he loved to play at parties, especially when inferiors were present, with high-keyed zest and malice. At home the daemon drove him to his desk; even in strange hotels he kept on scribbling, covering loose scraps of paper with his shaky, nondescript, block-letter hand.

One forgave Cal for much because one recognized the instability of his psyche. Madness never ceased to threaten him, and periodically it struck him down. In his twenties he had already perceived his fate:

Your lacerations tell the losing game
You play against a sickness past your cure.
How will the hands be strong? How will the heart endure?

For a while he sought refuge in the Church, but it failed him. Eros, who perennially beckoned, only reflected his mania, adding to his tumult. The two constants that he clung to, as elements of continuum in the precarious flux, were history and friendship, whose beauty is that they abide. "We are dear old friends," he would say at parting, with the stress on "old," as if time had managed to seal this covenant. Allen Tate, Randall Jarrell, Elizabeth Bishop, and Peter Taylor were even older friends, who had already been elevated, alive or dead, to angelic company. To him their works were sacred texts, though sometimes he would concede that even angels erred.

Most poets tend to resist criticism, and Lowell was no exception, fuming as others did about negative reviews. On the other hand, his method of composition was uniquely collaborative. He made his friends, willy-nilly, partners in his act, by showering them with early drafts of his poems, often so fragmentary and shapeless that it was no great trick to suggest improvements. Sometimes you saw a poem in half a dozen successive versions, each new version ampler and bolder than the last. You would recognize your own suggestions embedded in the text — a phrase here and there, a shift in the order of the lines — and you might wonder how many other hands had been involved in the process. It did not seem to matter much, for the end-product always presented itself as infallibly, unmistakably Lowellian. Even so, he kept modifying his poems each time they appeared in print. They were like the stream of Heraclitus: you could never dip into the same poem twice. Once the ghost of Jarrell appeared to him in a dream, scolding, "You didn't write, you *re*wrote." In a sense the representative voice of our age was a collective poet.

During the anguished period of his separation and divorce from Elizabeth Hardwick, I quarreled with him about the inclusion, in his poem, of raw material from her letters to him. It seemed to me a cruel invasion of her privacy, morally and aesthetically objectionable. In April 1972, after his alliance with Caroline Blackwood and the birth of their son Robert Sheridan, he wrote to me from Milgate Park, Kent, where they were living:

> Now full spring weather. Ivana [a stepdaughter] back at school. Sheridan eating everything in sight: blanket, rug, small dog, our fingers — a microcosm of James Dickey, but on the wagon. Lovely.
>
> About your criticism. I expect to be back in New York for a week beginning about the 21st of May, and hope to unwind over drinks with you. Dolphin is somewhat changed with the help of Elizabeth Bishop. The long birth sequence will come before the Flight to New York, a stronger conclusion, and one oddly softening the effect by giving a reason other than new love for my departure. Most of the letter poems — E.B.'s objection they were part fiction offered as truth — can go back to your old plan, a mixture of my voice, and another voice in my head, part me, part Lizzie, italicized, paraphrased, imperfectly, obsessively heard. I take it, it is these parts that repel you. I tried the new version out on Peter Taylor, and he couldn't imagine any moral objection to Dolphin. Not that the poem, alas, from its donnée, can fail to wound. *For Harriet and Lizzie* [sic] doesn't go with *History,* it goes before *Dolphin,* but I thought it was too sensational, *confessing,* to bring the two books out together. I think you are right, tho, and I'll do something. History

somehow echoes and stands aside from the other books. Do you think I could comb out enough excrescences from History to do much good? The metal too often reforged wears out. Maybe you could put your finger on a few of the worst. It must be as good almost as I can make it.

In November 1973, after the simultaneous publication, in three separate volumes, of *History, For Lizzie and Harriet,* and *The Dolphin,* Lowell gave a reading at the Pierpont Morgan Library in New York. What I said then, at the conclusion of my introduction of him, sums up my understanding of the nature and meaning of his achievement:

One of the disarming features of Lowell's work is that it does not pretend to aspire to the condition of an absolute art. He tells us the time in the right kind of voice for the day. He does not try to overpower us with a show of strength; instead, with his nervous vivacity, he hurries to build a chain of fortifications out of sand, or even dust. A revisionist by nature, he is forever tinkering with his old lines, rewriting his old poems, revamping his syntax, and periodically reordering his existence.

"It may be," he has remarked, "that some people have turned to my poems because of the very things that are wrong with me, I mean the difficulty I have with ordinary living, the impracticability, the myopia." Nobody else sounds quite like that. He makes us excruciatingly aware of the thrashing of the self behind the lines; of the intense fragility of the psyche trying to get a foothold in an "air of lost connections," struggling to stay human and alive. He is a poet who will even take the risk of sounding flat or dawdling in the hope of saying something true. What we get from these poems is the sense of a life . . . a life that has been turned into a style.

In the end the effort consumed him. He felt that he had turned, at the cost of his humanity, into a kind of literary monster, a machine for producing verse:

I have sat and listened to too many
words of the collaborating muse,

> and plotted perhaps too freely with my life,
> not avoiding injury to others,
> not avoiding injury to myself . . .

It had required an heroic endeavor to construct the strong persona of his poems: actually he had only a weak grip on his identity. In manic episodes he had confused himself with Christ, Saint Paul, and Hitler — particularly Hitler, whose dark spirit rose violently to possess him. Men of power had always fascinated him. Once, when I visited him at McLean's Hospital near Boston, he read "Lycidas" aloud to me, in his improved version, as if to assert his proprietary stake in the original.

Even his political convictions were more tentative than they appeared to be in his public statements. His eloquent rejection of President Johnson's invitation to the White House Arts Festival in 1965 had won him world-wide attention and had helped mobilize the forces of opposition to the Vietnam War, the forces that eventually brought Johnson down. Few realized that he had first accepted the invitation and then rescinded his acceptance at the urgent solicitation of a handful of friends. The name of Lowell was needed to catapult the story onto the front page of the *Times*. Politically and aesthetically a deep strain of conservatism opposed his liberal, humanitarian, and avant-garde leanings.

He had written of Flaubert, "the supreme artist," that "the mania for phrases enlarged his heart." Now the doctors had warned him that his own heart was dangerously enlarged. In *History* he had described his work as "this open book . . . my open coffin." The furious compulsion to tell his story pained and exhausted him. The ants were to be envied, for not being "under anathema to make it new." He longed to emulate Mallarmé, "who had the good fortune / to find a style that made writing impossible." Pound, Wilson, Auden, Berryman, Ransom were all freshly dead: "The old boys drop like wasps / from windowsill and pane." Both his parents, he chose to remember, had died of heart attacks at sixty. He hoped to die as insects do in mid-autumn, "instantly as one would ask of a friend."

He had his wish, dying at sixty, in a taxicab, on his way from
ennedy Airport after a flight from England. A fragment was found
mong his papers:

> Christ,
> may I die at night
> with a semblance of my senses
> like the full moon that fails.

Four days after Cal I arrived at Kennedy myself, on my return
om Italy. At the airport I called my wife, who filled in some
etails about the funeral arrangements. Then she added, "My sis-
r called last night from Chicago. She says we've lost a national
easure."

II

Toward the end of his life Robert Lowell made an effort, half
ffident, half magisterial — as became his nature — to sum up his
wn feelings about his achievement. "Looking over my *Selected
ems,*" he wrote,

> about thirty years of writing, my impression is that the thread
> that strings it together is my autobiography, it is a small-scale
> *Prelude,* written in many different styles and with digres-
> sions, yet a continuing story — still wayfaring. A story of
> what? Not the "growth of a poet's mind." Not a lesson and
> example to be handed to the student. Yet the mind must
> eventually age and grow, or the story would be a still-life,
> the pilgrimage of a zombi. My journey is always stumbling
> on the unforeseen and even unforeseeable. From year to year,
> things remembered from the past change almost more than
> the present.

He saw the past flowing into the present, the present interfusing
ith the past — always for him a fascinating turbulence. In a ner-
us jet of images, thoughts, sensations, he tried to convey the
brations of a life in its dangerous passage. One of his assump-
ns was that both pilgrim and landscape are fugitive, but he be-
ved in the consoling power of art and in its relative durability.
an age without a center and with little sense of direction he made

of his journey a symbolic action, speaking for us even in his stum
bling. Fame did not modify his nature — he always expected
be famous. Money and family gave him advantages, of which I
was well aware, but one of his differences from other poets wa
that he worked harder at his poems than anybody else did. Ever
day of his life was a day for poetry. At sixty, when his heart gav
out, he was still quizzical, vulnerable, obsessive.

The world that flattered Lowell and, in its grosser manifesta
tion, envied him had little understanding of the anguish at the co
of his experience. Perhaps his greatest triumph, in the face of ba
terings that would have paralyzed others, was the creation of tl
strong persona that animates the body of his work. Many of h
most celebrated poems had their origins in manic episodes, the wi
ejaculations being gradually hammered into shape as his min
cleared. He came to believe that people responded to his work b
cause they recognized, in the projections of his damaged psych
their own flaws.

In the twentieth century we prefer to think of our poets as rel
els and innovators, and it is not absurd to fit Lowell into the
categories. Nevertheless, he remained very much a traditionalis
nourished by his New England roots, steeped in the classic
preoccupied with technique, shored up by Christian and pos
Christian values. He loved the drama of history and fed his imag
ination on its march and panoply and terror. His historical co
sciousness heightened his awareness of human transience and
the artist's need to document his fleeting appearance on the scen

> We are poor passing facts,
> warned by that to give
> each figure in the photograph
> his living name.

"In life," he once said,

> we speak with many false voices; occasionally, if we are lucky,
> we find a true one in our poems. A poem needs to include
> man's contradictions. One side of me, for example, is a con-
> ventional liberal, concerned with causes, agitated about peace

and justice and equality, as many people are. My other side is deeply conservative, wanting to get at the roots of things, wanting to slow down the whole modern process of mechanization and dehumanization, knowing that liberalism can be a form of death too. In the writing of a poem all our compulsions and biases should get in, so that finally we don't know what we mean.

If he had been less of a traditionalist, his intermittent radical decisions and statements, including his stand as a conscientious objector in World War II (for which he went to jail), his celebrated rebuff to President Johnson on the occasion of the disastrous White House Arts Festival, his march on the Pentagon in support of a generation's rejection of the Vietnam War, his outcry against political imprisonment, his warnings of nuclear holocaust, would have impressed us less. Though he was not a man of action, he had a great intuitive gift for significant gesture. And though he was more deeply committed to the past than most contemporaries, the quick touch of his poetry was on the nerve of the modern.

Though Lowell wrote in a succession of styles, indicative of his mercurial temperament, each phase carried his unmistakable signature. Technical problems engaged his attention and never ceased to excite him. He could wax eloquent in conversation on a question of prosodic substitutions or the applicability of quantitative verse to English metrics. In his early verse, as in "The Quaker Graveyard in Nantucket," conceived as a Miltonic elegy for his cousin Warren Winslow, who died at sea during World War II, he wielded a heavy iambic hammer capable of striking the magnificent resonances demanded by his apocalyptic vision. At this stage, culminating in the appearance of *Lord Weary's Castle,* published when he was not yet thirty, Lowell was a "fire-breathing" Catholic convert — though not for long. His poetry reflected his zeal.

For *Life Studies,* perhaps the most influential book of modern verse since *The Waste Land,* precipitating a flood of "confessional" poetry, most of which he scorned, Lowell found his model in Flaubert, a prosy style suitable for autobiography and reminiscence, replete with "ironic or amusing particulars." Looking back on this volume, Lowell recalled with relish, "I did all kinds of tricks with meter and the avoidance of meter." In *For the Union Dead* he reverted to strict meter, yet tried to avoid "the symbols and heroics" of his first books. The eight-line stanza in tetrameter couplets that he borrowed from Andrew Marvell for *Near the Ocean* seemed to him "Godsent," the precisely right medium for handling national events. He described himself as "almost breathing couplets all one summer and deep into the next autumn." Then for six years, in the making of *Notebook* (rechristened *History* when revised and expanded), he wrote unrhymed blank verse sonnets, until he grew weary of the "cramping and military beat" and turned, at the last, to unrhymed free verse.

Most of Lowell's poems — with the conspicuous exception of those in *Life Studies* — are difficult to grasp at a hearing. By and large, despite his concern with technique, he did not write for the ear. He tended to follow Keats's precept of loading every rift with ore. His lines are crammed with details of perception, speculation, information, but far from dwelling on them, he was characteristically impatient to push on. He was congenitally predisposed to produce a poetry that moves with the velocity of a mountain torrent, precipitating silt and stones down into the valley. During one of his readings he remarked, somewhat ruefully, that he was reminded of Santayana's comment that the man on the platform goes racing ahead on horseback while the audience tries vainly to catch up with him on foot.

His speaking voice, he realized, with its New England nasal twang and lack of expressive range, was not an ideal instrument. The poet, in his own phrase, "hums the auditorium dead." In order to liven the proceedings he became increasingly discursive at his readings, sandwiching his poems between thick layers of explanation and anecdote. At his best, when he was relaxed and confident, as in his 1960 reading at the Library of Congress, he was able to captivate his audience with his wit and charm and the elegance of his commentary. These prose interludes, as recorded on tape, contribute to an understanding of his art and a sense of his living presence.

Lowell had once remarked that "writing is neither transport nor a technique." In his last effort to say something more definitive about his lifework he stressed what he perceived to be the limits of his enterprise: "What I write almost always comes out of the pressure of some inner concern, temptation or obsessive puzzle. . . . All my poems are written for catharsis; none can heal melancholia or arthritis." But he would not deny that he had reached for a grander prize: "I pray that my progress has been more than recoiling with satiation and disgust from one style to another, a series of rebuffs. I hope there has been increase of beauty, wisdom, tragedy, and all the blessings of this consuming chance."

THE WISDOM OF THE BODY

A poem is at once the most primitive and most sophisticated use of language, but my emphasis is on the former as the more significant attribute. The priest or shaman of the tribe casting his spell over things was close to the roots of the poetic experience. Any child who has ever poised a ladybug on his fingertip and advised it, with a solicitous puff of breath, to "fly away home, your house is on fire and your children all gone," has unwittingly participated in an ancient ritual associated with a portentously sacred event. Variations of that precautionary incantation survive in all parts of the world, in at least a dozen different tongues, subject to interpretation as remnants of the worship of the sun, or Isis, or Mary, et al. The words of a poem go back to the beginnings of the human adventure when the first symbols were not spoken but sung or chanted or danced.

Poetry is not to be confused with writing, any more than it is to be confused with rhyme or versification. In the experience of the race, poetry must be millions of years old, but writing is a comparatively recent invention. The Sumerians incised their first cuneiform tablets around 4000 B.C., followed about a millennium later by the Egyptians with their hieroglyphs. Story-telling cultures had long been in existence, but people did not put their stories into writing or inscribe thoughts and feelings until near Homer's time, less than three thousand years ago.

Now for ages before that, "immense quantities of human experience," in Alfred North Whitehead's phrase, "had been accumulating in men's bodies." The body, in its genetic code, holds the long odyssey of the race. When our organs are working healthily and harmoniously, the joy that floods our being cannot be much ifferent from what Adam knew. No interpreter is needed for a onversation between bodies. As is represented in the story of the ower of Babel, the peoples of the earth are separated by their languages, but they are brought together, in common understanding, y a universal language of gesture. Gestural language antedates erbal languages, and some symbolic gestures link us with the animal kingdom, as when we avert our eyes and neck in an attitude f submission, stamp our feet in rage, or nod our heads in the act f greeting.

From recent studies of the evolution of the brain, we learn that he forebrain, the neocortex, is the organ of philosophy and the ciences; but poems rise out of the swamps of the hindbrain, "the ld brain," dragging their amphibian memories behind them. The words of a poem are charged with the wisdom of the body and if hey are trapped into print they jump from the page, because they re so vibrant with gesture.

That physical, even animal, source of poetry is reflected in one f Ben Jonson's observations. "A rimer and a poet are two things," e wrote. "It is said of the incomparable Virgil that he brought orth his verses like a bear, and after formed them with licking."

In the physicality of the medium we find an explanation of our inesthetic response to poetry, the sort of response that Emily Dickinson proposed as her litmus test: "If I read a book and it makes my whole body so cold no fire can ever warm me, I know that is poetry. If I feel physically as if the top of my head were taken off, know that is poetry."

Alluding to the effect of poetry, A. E. Housman recalled the words of Eliphaz the Temanite, who was one of Job's comforters: "A spirit passed before my face; the hair of my flesh stood up." "Experience has taught me," continued Housman, "when I am having of a morning, to keep watch over my thoughts, because, a line of poetry strays into my memory, my skin bristles so that he razor ceases to act. This particular symptom is accompanied y a shiver down the spine; there is another which consists of a onstriction of the throat; and there is a third which I can only describe by borrowing a phrase from one of Keats's last letter where he says, speaking of Fanny Brawne, 'everything that r minds me of her goes through me like a spear.' The seat of th sensation is the pit of the stomach."

Blake taught us that the chief inlets of soul are the five sense Certainly the chief inlet of poetry is through the ear. A poem mu be felt to be understood, and before it can be felt it must be hear Poets listen for their poems, and we, as readers, must listen in tur If we listen hard enough, who knows? — we too may break in dance, perhaps for grief, perhaps for joy.

When I am asked by young poets what advice I have to off them about the conduct of their lives, I am inclined to warn the about the dangers of hothouse anemia. "Do something else," I te them, "develop any other skill, turn to any other branch knowledge. Learn how to use your hands. Try woodworking, bir watching, gardening, sailing, weaving, pottery, archaeolog oceanography, spelunking, animal husbandry — take your pic Whatever activity you engage in, as trade or hobby or field stud will tone up your body and clear your head. At the very least will help you with your metaphors."

Although poetry as a technique insists on particulars, on spec ficity of perception, the poet in his vocation is not a specialist bu as Wordsworth understood, a generalist, a person speaking to pe sons. The poet speaks to others not only through what he says b through what he is, his symbolic presence, as though he carried set of flags reading Have a Heart, Let Nothing Get By, Live at t Center of Your Being. His life instructs us that it is not necessar or even desirable, for everyone to join the crowds streaming on the professional or business highways, pursuing the bitch go dess.

I think of William Blake warning us that "A dog starv'd at h master's gate / Predicts the ruin of the state"; of John Keats changin into the sparrow that came to peck on his windowsill; of Gera Manley Hopkins lamenting, when an ashtree in the seminary ga den at Stoneyhurst had been chopped down, "I wished to die ar

[52]

not to see the inscapes of the world destroyed any more"; of William Butler Yeats in his old age, "a tattered coat upon a stick," confiding to a younger woman, "I am writing poetry . . . and as always happens, no matter how I begin, it becomes love poetry before I am finished with it."

"This is what you shall do," wrote Walt Whitman in his preface to *Leaves of Grass:*

> Love the earth and sun and the animals, despise riches, give alms to every one that asks, stand up for the stupid and crazy, devote your income and labour to others, hate tyrants, argue not concerning God, have patience and indulgence toward the people, take off your hat to nothing known or unknown, or to any man or number of men — go freely with powerful uneducated persons, and with the young, and with the mothers of families — re-examine all you have been told in school or church or in any book, and dismiss whatever insults your own soul; and your very flesh shall be a great poem, and have the richest fluency, not only in its words, but in the silent lines of its lips and face, and between the lashes of your eyes, and in every motion and joint of your body.

We need to refrain, as Walt Whitman does, from speaking of mind as though it were somehow opposed to body, or of spirit as though it were somehow superior to mind. In my philosophy, all three — body, mind, spirit — are merely stages of incandescence, or awareness, in the same living organism. As the lights go on within, we begin to see everything that is, everything that happens, impinging on us. Our most sublime thoughts have their feet planted in clay; our best songs are body-songs.

AT THE TOMB OF WALT WHITMAN

> Behold! I do not give lectures, or a
> little charity;
> When I give, I give myself.

In my youth, let me confess, I condescended to Walt Whitman. Compared to the Metaphysical poets who first enchanted me, he seemed windy, boastful, coarse-grained, shapeless, inelegant. It took me years to realize that however true, or partly true, these strictures may be, the missing perception is that the greatness triumphs over the flaws, makes quibbles out of them.

To be an American poet at all it is essential, in the course of a lifetime, to come to terms with the "hankering, gross, mystical, nude" giant who bestrides our literature. As early as 1916 Ezra Pound had arrived at this understanding of his predecessor, in full awareness of their differences. The lines of his apologia are familiar, but worth repeating:

> I make a pact with you, Walt Whitman —
> I have detested you long enough.
> I come to you as a grown child
> Who has had a pig-headed father;
> I am old enough now to make friends.
> It was you that broke the new wood.
> Now it is time for carving.
> We have one sap and one root —
> Let there be commerce between us.

The more commerce we have with Walt Whitman, the more he eludes us. No writer has talked so much about himself and left the

[54]

sources of his genius so inexplicable. Nothing in his background or early history marks him as one destined for immortality. His mother, who doted on him no less than he doted on her — to the day of her death he remained mama's boy — was practically illiterate. His morose father was an unsuccessful carpenter and builder. Of the eight Whitman children who survived infancy (Walt was the second), four had serious mental or psychological disabilities — one in fact died in an insane asylum, another as an alcoholic. Walt's formal schooling ended at the age of eleven in Brooklyn, where the family had settled for a while after moving from Long Island. Until the publication of *Leaves of Grass* in 1855, in his thirty-sixth year, he had drifted from job to job as printer, country schoolmaster, journalist, and newspaper editor; had written some excruciatingly sentimental fiction, and composed occasional and patriotic verses of no merit whatsoever.

Meanwhile secretly, underground, so to speak, he was preparing himself for his task, waiting for the moment when he would be ready to emerge from his chrysalis. Perhaps Emerson had given him the clue to his assignment when he announced: "America is a poem in our eyes; its ample geography dazzles the imagination, and it will not wait long for metres." Emerson had also said: "The world is young. We too must write Bibles, to unite again the heavens and the earthly worlds."

Whitman accepted the challenge. He would write the epic poem that America lacked, he would give it the unifying song that a great civilization requires; the Spirit of Democracy would be its sustaining myth, and he — Walt Whitman — would be its hero, standing not for himself alone, but as an embodiment of a whole people. "The United States themselves are essentially the greatest poem," he affirmed in his preface to *Leaves of Grass,* no doubt deliberately echoing Emerson.

> Walt Whitman am I — a Kosmos, of mighty Manhat-
> tan the son,
> Turbulent, fleshy and sensual, eating, drinking and
> breeding;

No sentimentalist — no stander above men and women,
	or apart from them;
No more modest than immodest. . . .

I speak the pass-word primeval — I give the sign of
	democracy;
By God! I will accept nothing which all cannot have
	their counterpart of on the same terms.

Through me many long dumb voices;
Voices of prostitutes, and of deform'd persons;
Voices of the diseas'd and despairing, and of thieves and
	dwarfs;
Voices of cycles of preparation and accretion,
And of the threads that connect the stars — and wombs
	and of the father-stuff,
And of the rights of them the others are down upon;
Of the trivial, flat, foolish, despised,
Fog in the air, beetles rolling balls of dung.

Through me forbidden voices;
Voices of sexes and lusts — voices veil'd, and I remove
	the veil;
Voices indecent, by me clarified and transfigur'd. . . .

I believe in the flesh and the appetites;
Seeing, hearing, feeling, are miracles, and each part and
	tag of me is a miracle.

Divine am I inside and out, and I make holy whatever
	I touch or am touch'd from;
The scent of these arm-pits, aroma finer than prayer;
This head more than churches, bibles, and all the creeds.

One of the wonders of Whitman's self-defining Cosmos is how
much wilderness it contains. The lost and the rejected, inseparable
from elements of his own nature, are everywhere folded into his
embrace. Despite the compelling sanity of his presence, there are
times when one suspects he must have been only a step away from
babbling, or Chaos. ("You villain touch! what are you doing? My

breath is tight in its throat; / Unclench your floodgates! you are too much for me.") What saved him was that he had set his heart on Mythos, the far country toward which he sailed. In order to get there he had to transform himself. This is the supreme and imperative act of the poetic imagination: to create the person who will write the poems. It was for him an heroic enterprise.

> I am the poet of the Body and I am the poet of the Soul,
> The pleasures of heaven are with me and the pains of
>   hell are with me,
> The first I graft and increase upon myself, the latter I
>   translate into a new tongue.
>
> I am the poet of the woman the same as the man,
> And I say it is as great to be a woman as to be a man,
> And I say there is nothing greater than the mother of
>   men. . . .
>
> Prodigal, you have given me love — therefore I to you
>   give love!
> O unspeakable passionate love.

When we try to isolate the influences that contributed to Whitman's process of transformation, we are confounded by their multiplicity. Among them was his enthusiasm for the spellbinding oratory of the Quaker preacher Elias Hicks, from whom he accepted the doctrine of the Inner Light and the conviction that every man was his own temple and priest. On the verge of identifying himself as a Hicksite Quaker, he was wary enough to draw back, noting, "I was never made to live inside a fence."

Few young men of his time could have been such omnivorous readers: the world's literature became his university. As book reviewer for the *Brooklyn Eagle* he wrote about Carlyle, Coleridge, Goethe, George Sand, Schlegel, and a host of others, without ever seeming at a loss for words or opinions. His comment on Coleridge has a prophetic ring to it: "We think this man stands above all poets. He was passionate without being morbid — he was like

Adam in Paradise, and almost as free from artificiality" — sentiments that must have corresponded with his own burgeoning aspiration.

As he set to work on *Leaves of Grass* he felt that he was present at the original act of creation and that he shared the divine principle:

> I believe a leaf of grass is no less than the journey-work
>   of the stars
> And the pismire is equally perfect, and a grain of sand,
>   and the egg of the wren,
> And the tree-toad is a chef d'oeuvre for the highest,
> And the running blackberry would adorn the parlors of
>   heaven.

He had that quality of empathy, that ability to flow into others, to be everything and nothing without irritable striving that Keats defined as Negative Capability, the mark of the Poetical Character. When Whitman came across that eloquent passage in Keats's letters, he underlined it.

In "Song of Myself" we observe him passing through mineral, vegetable, and animal states of being:

> I find I incorporate gneiss, coal, long-threaded moss,
>   fruits, grains, esculent roots,
> And am stucco'd with quadrupeds and birds all over.

His praise of the animal kingdom is leavened by a touch of humor:

> I think I could turn and live with animals, they are so
>   placid and self-contain'd;
> I stand and look at them long and long.
> They do not sweat and whine about their condition;
> They do not lie awake in the dark and weep for their
>   sins;
> They do not make me sick discussing their duty to God.

Sometimes he identifies himself with Christ, sharing His agonies; more often he assumes the form of a vegetation god, Osiris or Dionysus, enduring the cycles of death and rebirth. Egyptology, it should be noted, was one of his favorite studies. He frequently visited on Broadway Dr. Henry Abbott's pioneering exhibition of Egyptian antiquities and wrote an article about it.

The grass was for him a "hieroglyphic," which he deciphered as saying to him, "All goes onward and outward, nothing collapses, / And to die is different from what any one supposed, and luckier."

> Scented herbage of my breast,
> Leaves from you I glean, I write, to be perused best
>   afterwards,
> Tomb-leaves, body-leaves growing up above me above
>   death . . .

Those images are straight from the representations (familiar to Whitman) of Osiris, the slain god, with verdure sprouting from his breast.

Limitless fertility. Universal love. Bacchic joys. In *Leaves of Grass* the gender of lover and beloved is interchangeably male and female. My intuition is that Whitman had to recognize and accept his own androgyny before he was able to identify with the vegetation god whose ritual death and rebirth he enacts and celebrates. In Greek myth the polymorphous aspect of the god of wine and fertility is underscored. Dionysus was raised in the women's quarters. A frenzied band of women were the chief celebrants of his ecstatic rites, and he himself was capable of assuming female form. In Euripides' *Bacchae* the god's double, Pentheus, is slain while dressed as a woman.

"I sing the Body electric," cried Walt.

> O my Body! I dare not desert the likes of you in other
>   men and women, nor the likes of the parts of
>   you;

> I believe the likes of you are to stand or fall with the
> likes of the Soul, (and that they are the Soul)
> I believe the likes of you shall stand or fall with my
> poems — and that they are poems,
> Man's, woman's, child's, youth's, wife's, husband's,
> mother's, father's, young man's, young wom-
> an's poems.

The only comparable modern effort to create a universal epic protagonist, a collective persona, is to be found in Joyce's *Finnegans Wake,* but it must be said that Humphrey Chimpden Earwicker, HCE, Here Comes Everybody, being primarily a product of the linguistic imagination, has weaker vital emanations than Walt's astonishingly robust pansexual creation.

I am not implying that Whitman was indifferent to the possibilities of language. On the contrary, he was passionately, scrupulously committed to inventing a language adequate to his ambition.

> Speech is the twin of my vision — it is unequal to
> measure itself;
> It provokes me forever;
> It says sarcastically, *Walt, you contain enough — why don't
> you let it out then?*

"Great is language," he declared, "it is the mightiest of sciences." He applied himself to the study of historical linguistics under the tutelage of a professor of ancient and modern languages. Words, he asserted, were "metaphysical beings. . . . A perfect writer would make words sing, dance, kiss, do the male and female act, bear children . . . or do anything that man or woman or the natural powers can do."

He sought for words that would match his evolving identity, such words as "robust, brawny, athletic, muscular . . . resistance, bracing, rude, rugged, rough, shaggy, bearded, arrogant, haughty." He made a list of his key words in "An American

Primer," a gathering of notes for a public lecture on language, and he pronounced them "alive and sinewy — they walk, look, step with an air of command."

Indeed, once he described *Leaves of Grass* as "only a language experiment . . . an attempt to give the spirit, the body, the man, new words, new potentialities of speech. . . .

"The English language," he maintained, "befriends the grand American expression. . . . It is the powerful language of resistance . . . it is the dialect of common sense. It is the speech of the proud and melancholy races and all who aspire. It is the chosen tongue to express growth faith self-esteem freedom justice equality friendliness amplitude prudence decision and courage. It is the medium that shall well nigh express the inexpressible."

In order to forge a language appropriate for his new Democratic Bible, Whitman found it necessary to jettison the metrical and prosodic conventions of the period, along with the polite themes and vocabulary that complied with the decorum of an age.

Certainly his cadences, his rolling periods, his parallel constructions are heavily indebted to the Bible, particularly the Psalms, the Song of Solomon, and the books of the prophets — but they are not slavish imitations. The inflection is freshly modern, not archaic. His own stamp is on every page.

Another of his sources was oratory, a pervasive influence in an epoch of exalted public rhetoric, political as well as religious. Several years after his exposure to the rhapsodies of Elias Hicks, Whitman heard the famous sailor-preacher Father Taylor (Father Mapple in *Moby Dick*) and was moved to comment: "When Father Taylor preach'd or pray'd, the rhetoric and art, the mere words (which usually play such a big part) seem'd altogether to disappear, and the *live feeling* advanced upon you and seiz'd you with a power before unknown."

That description provides an insight into the nature of Whitman's own art, with its incremental rhythms, sweeping gestures, and copious draughts of live feeling.

"But for the opera," Whitman once reflected, "I could never have written *Leaves of Grass*," and it is undeniable that Italian opera, to which he became fervently addicted in the early 1850s, contributed to the liberation of his rhetoric. Words such as *aria, cantabile, recitative* crept into his vocabulary and, as compositional strategies, modified his style. His poetry became, in a sense, operatic, generously expressive at its best, florid and overbearing at its worst.

He felt that there was nothing more spiritual and at the same time more sensuous than music. One of his provocative observations was that "music, in the legitimate sense of that term, exists independently of technical music . . . just as poetry exists independently of rhyme." His love of music gave him an insight into the nature of poetry that was to lead to a central pronouncement in his preface to *Leaves of Grass:* "The poetic quality is not marshalled in rhyme or uniformity or abstract addresses to things nor in melancholy complaints or good precepts, but is the life of these and much else and is in the soul. . . . The rhyme and uniformity of perfect poems show the free growth of metrical laws and bud from them as unerringly and loosely as lilacs or roses on a bush, and take shapes as compact as the shapes of chestnuts and oranges and melons and pears, and shed the perfume impalpable to form."

Whitman's statement is worthy of standing side by side with Coleridge's classic formulation of the concept of organic, as opposed to mechanic, form: "The organic form . . . is innate; it shapes and it develops itself from within, and the fullness of its development is one and the same with the perfection of its outward form."

Eighty-five years after the publication of *Leaves of Grass,* in a letter to a wealthy friend, Wallace Stevens proposed the endowment of a chair for the study of poetry. "What is intended," he explained, "is to study the theory of poetry in relation to what poetry has been and in relation to what it ought to be. Its literature is a part of it, and only a part of it. For this purpose, poetry means not the language of poetry but the thing itself, wherever it may be found. It does not mean verse any more than philosophy means prose. . . ."

Long before Whitman or Stevens, the twelfth-century Chinese poet Yang Wan-li, one of the Four Masters of Southern Sung Poetry, addressed his disciples in the wake of his experience of "enlightenment." This is what he said: "Now, what is poetry? If you say it is simply a matter of words, I will say, 'A good poet gets rid of words.' If you say it is simply a matter of meaning, I will say, 'A good poet gets rid of meaning.' But you will say, if words and meanings are gotten rid of, where is the poetry? To this I reply, 'Get rid of words and meaning, and there is still poetry.' "

An enigmatic utterance, but I doubt that either Whitman or Stevens would have been baffled by it. On the surface they would seem to be incompatible poets, but like Pound before him, Stevens too had come to terms with his progenitor. "In the far South," he wrote, "the sun of autumn is passing"

> Like Walt Whitman walking along a ruddy shore.
> He is singing and chanting the things that are part of
> him,
> The words that were and will be, death and day.
> Nothing is final, he chants. No man shall see the end.
> His beard is of fire and his staff is a leaping flame.

"Great are the myths," proclaimed Whitman — "I too delight in them." He took special delight in the myth of himself, the godlike one sounding his "barbaric yawp over the roofs of the world." "I am by no means the benevolent, equable, happy creature you portray," he confessed to his friend and biographer Dr. Richard Maurice Bucke, "but let that pass — I have left it as you wrote."

He was insecure financially and emotionally; his history of publication was an unmitigated disaster; his ruddy health failed him in middle life and left him a paralyzed old man; he felt (for good cause) neglected by his countrymen, though he had his devotees and a good measure of international fame; love was offered to him that he was unable to respond to, and he knew in turn the pangs of unrequited love; he had sung the glories of America the beautiful, and he felt that vision betrayed by a pack of scoundrels.

[63]

After the assassination of his beloved President, in the midst of the Reconstruction period, he raged that American society was "canker'd, crude, superstitious, and rotten." The vehemence of his indictment still burns on the page:

Never was there, perhaps, more hollowness of heart than at present, and here in the United States. Genuine belief seems to have left us. . . . We live in an atmosphere of hypocrisy throughout. . . . The depravity of the business classes of our country is not less than has been supposed, but infinitely greater. The official services of America, national, state, and municipal, in all their branches and departments, except the judiciary, are saturated in corruption, bribery, falsehood, mal-administration; and the judiciary is tainted. The great cities reek with respectable as much as non-respectable robbery and scoundrelism. . . . The best class we show is but a mob of fashionably dress'd speculators and vulgarians. . . . I say that our New World democracy . . . is, so far, an almost complete failure. . . .

He who had proclaimed America's Manifest Destiny and invoked divine support for our imperial ambitions was forced to concede: "In vain have we annex'd Texas, California, Alaska, and reach north for Canada and south for Cuba. It is as if we were somehow being endow'd with a vast and more and more thoroughly-appointed body, and then left with little or no soul.

"The history of Democracy," he concluded, "remains unwritten, because that history has yet to be enacted."

There had been a time when, despite adversity, he had exuded self-confidence, self-esteem, superlative health, an unquenchable lovingkindness of spirit. During wartime in Washington he had walked slowly through the ghastly hospital wards, through the long corridors of blood and pain, like a ministering angel — comforting, consoling, embracing, kissing the sick and the dying.

The naturalist John Burroughs, a proper married man, was innocently enthralled by the plenitude of this demiurge, his amazing friend. "I love him very much," wrote Burroughs from the capital. "He loves everything and everybody. I saw a soldier the other day stop on the street and kiss him. He kisses me as if I were a girl. . . . He bathed today while I was there — such a handsome body, and such delicate and rosy flesh I never saw before. I told him he looked good enough to eat."

His best-kept secret was the degree of his self-doubt and perturbation, the dark fears that beset him. Over the span of years he had been a tireless publicist of his genius, composing dozens of unsigned reviews that never stinted in their praise. Toward the last, in a widely reprinted article that he wrote anonymously for a Camden newspaper, he summed up his career as though it were a dismal failure, at least in terms of recognition and rewards. It may be that he was indulging in deliberate exaggeration, as a stratagem for exciting sympathy and selling books, when he described himself, in the third person, at the age of fifty-six, as living obscurely and neglected, "old, poor, and paralyzed"; but the tone of bitterness and frustration comes through as genuine.

Whitman's poems, he declared, "have fallen stillborn in this country. They have been met, and are met today, with the determined denial, disgust and scorn of orthodox American authors, publishers and editors, and, in a pecuniary and worldly sense, have certainly wrecked the life of their author."

The poet who walked in sunlight and boundless optimism had always gone to sleep with an antithetical self. From his childhood, Death was ever a companion presence, threatening him and those closest to him, the ineluctable antagonist, but yet oddly seductive, an object of yearning.

> A word then, (for I will conquer it,)
> The word final, superior to all,
> Subtle, sent up — what is it? — I listen;
> Are you whispering it, and have been all the time, you
>   sea-waves?
> Is that it from your liquid rims and wet sands?
>
> Whereto answering, the sea,
> Delaying not, hurrying not,

Whisper'd me through the night, and very plainly be-
fore daybreak,
Lisp'd to me the low and delicious word DEATH;
And again Death — ever Death, Death, Death,
Hissing melodious, neither like the bird, nor like my
arous'd child's heart,
But edging near, as privately for me, rustling at my feet,
Creeping thence steadily up to my ears, and laving me
softly all over,
Death, Death, Death, Death, Death.

Which I do not forget,
But fuse the song of my dusky demon and brother,
That he sang to me in the moonlight on Paumanok's
gray beach,
With the thousand responsive songs, at random,
My own songs, awaked from that hour;
And with them the key, the word up from the waves,
The word of the sweetest song, and all songs,
That strong and delicious word which, creeping to my
feet,
The sea whisper'd me.

In poem after poem he practiced how to dissipate his fear: Death
became for him the supreme transforming power of the Universe,
magical, imperial, triumphant, but infinitely tender, embracing, the
grandest and mightiest of all the manifestations of Democracy. His
songs of Democracy and Death blended; they made a contrapuntal
music, culminating in the matchless hymn that celebrated his fallen
hero, "When Lilacs Last in the Dooryard Bloom'd."

When the time came for him to prepare for his own death and
the disposal of his remains, he knew how to make the most of it,
enlarging on the simple instructions he had written years before:
"I bequeathe myself to the dirt, to grow from the grass I love; / If
you want me again, look for me under your bootsoles."

He ordered a monumental burial vault, cut into the hillside of
Harleigh Cemetery in Camden, faced with marble and tile, and

big enough to hold eventually the rest of his family, though only his name announces who is buried there. The design of the tomb itself, "a massive stone temple," built of rough Quincy granite, he borrowed from one of William Blake's symbolic etchings, *Death's Door*. The great blocks weigh as much as ten tons apiece; the roof is a foot and a half thick. Whitman described it with pride as "the rudest most undress'd structure . . . since Egypt, perhaps the cave dwellers."

While the tomb was under construction, its eventual occupant gloried in its magnificence, visited it regularly with his friends in his horse-carriage, and picnicked on the grounds.

He had signed a contract to pay $4000 — a fortune in those days — on the completion of his mausoleum. When the staggering bill came due, one of his friends had to come to his rescue to satisfy the debt. As with so many other details of the biography, this one is beyond either laughter or tears. Indeed, Whitman's life as a whole cannot be viewed, in classic perspective, as either comedy or tragedy — it partakes in full measure of both.

That burial place of his choosing is still rustic, careless in its beauty, impinging on the wild. A few years ago, on an anniversary occasion, when I stood there, in Camden's Harleigh Cemetery, and read aloud from his poems to a small band of his disciples, I sensed the rightness of his identification with the earth-force, the divinity of the seed, and I thought for a moment I understood why his poems survive, in keeping with his prophecy, as "tomb-leaves, body-leaves growing up above me above death."

THE LAYERS
Some Notes on "The Abduction" *

A few months ago a graduate student at a midwestern university sent me an elaborate commentary on an early poem of mine, requesting my seal of approval for his interpretation. Since I could scarcely recall the lines in question — they had been produced in my twenties — I needed first of all to reacquaint myself with them, almost as if they had been written by a stranger. Something quite disturbing happened to me. As I began to read, the apparent subject matter crumbled away, and what I heard was a cry out of the past, evoking images of an unhappy time, the pang of a hopeless love affair, in a rush of memory that clouded the page. When I turned to my correspondent's thesis, I found that a large portion of it was devoted to an analysis and classification of prosodic devices, fortifying his perception of the poem as an example of metaphysical wit. Such discrepancies are not isolated occurrences. The readers of a poem perceive it as a verbal structure, about which they are free to speculate; whereas the poet himself is irrevocably bound to the existential source.

Even with the advantage of inside knowledge, including specific information about the occasions and intentions of what he has written, the poet is less likely than his critics to assume that he fully understands the operations of the creative faculty. Reason certainly enters into the work of the imagination, but the work has its own reasons. In my later years I have wanted to write poems that are simple on the surface, even transparent in their diction, but without denying that much of the power of poetry has its

*See "The Abduction," page 4.

origins in the secrecy of the life and in the evocativeness of language itself, which is anciently deep in mysteries.

One of the great resources of the poetic imagination is its capacity to mount thought on thought, event on event, image on image, time on time, a process that I term "layering." The life of the mind is largely a buried life. That is why the ideal imagination, namely, the Shakespearean one, can be compared to Jerusalem or Rome, cities sacred and eternal, great capitals built on their ruins, mounted on successive layers of civilization.

To a poet of my age each new poem presents itself in a double aspect, as a separate entity demanding to be perfected and, conversely, as an extension of the lifework, to which it is joined by invisible psychic filaments. In this latter aspect, all the poems of a lifetime can be said to add up to a single poem . . . one that is never satisfied with itself, never finished.

Poems do not want to explain themselves, even to the mind that makes them. Those most deeply embedded in the history of the self are the most reluctant to betray their ancestry and motivations. They seem to come out of nowhere — a gift, to be sure, for which one ought to be thankful, but delivered suspiciously without a postmark and wrapped in bafflement.

Ostensibly "The Abduction" began for me in Provincetown, Massachusetts, in the middle of a summer night when I woke and turned to gaze on the face of my sleeping wife: "You lie beside me in elegant repose, / a hint of transport hovering on your lips." In the actual writing, these were my first lines. Some thirty years before, in another place and a different life, a similar circumstance had engendered the opening of "The Science of the Night":

> I touch you in the night, whose gift was you,
> My careless sprawler,
> And I touch you cold, unstirring, star-bemused,
> That have become the land of your self-strangeness.

It strikes me that in both "The Science of the Night" and "The Abduction," the epithet for the body abandoned to its night-self

[69]

is "indifferent," a word less accusatory than poignant, born of the knowledge that when we are most ourselves, as in sleep, we are most withdrawn from others, even those we love. That capacity for withdrawal may be one of the conditions of the creative life.

In this connection I am reminded of a passage in one of Henry James's late letters, as eloquent as it is revealing:

"The port from which I set out was, I think, that of the *essential loneliness of my life* — and it seems to me the port, in sooth, to which again finally my course directs itself. This loneliness (since I mention it!) — what is it still but the deepest thing about one? Deeper about me, at any rate, than anything else, deeper than my 'genius,' deeper than my 'discipline,' deeper than my pride, deeper above all than the deep counter-minings of art."

When I review the genesis of "The Abduction," its subterranean strategies ("counter-minings," in James's phrase), I see that there are two women in the poem, maybe three, combined into a single figure. The image of the woman stumbling out of the woods came to me in a dream, just as I have recorded it, two or three months after I had put aside, in discouragement, my initial lines. Physically she resembled the "careless sprawler" of "The Science of the Night," who had kept a guilty secret from me; but the scenario of her fantastic adventure clearly derived from a book I had been reading, written by a friend, about UFO abductions.* One of the documents in the book is the transcript of an hypnotic session with a subject named Virginia, detailing her encounter in a glade with "a beautiful deer . . . a mystical deer." I might add that among the books of my youth that fired my imagination were Grimm's fairy tales, Ovid's *Metamorphoses,* Bulfinch's mythologies, and *Gawain and the Green Knight.* Shape-shifting remains for me a viable metaphor.

In the vaults of memory everything unforgotten is equally real. Echoes of what we have read, dreamed, or imagined co-exist in the mind with remembrances of "actual" happenings. The experience of poetry itself is part of the reality that enters into the making

Missing Time, by Budd Hopkins (New York: Richard Marek, 1981).

of a poem. I venture that there is a connection, however tenuous, between my account of "the engines of the night thrumming" and Milton's mysterious evocation, in "Lycidas," of "that two-handed engine at the door," but I doubt that anyone else would even guess at the linkage. Somewhat more palpable, I suppose, is the rhythmic allusion, at the end of my poem, to Yeats's celebrated question, "How can we know the dancer from the dance?"

"The Abduction" came to me, in all its aspects, as a poem of transformation. Once the transforming spirit had asserted itself, a host of preternatural images, not all of which I can identify, arrived in a cluster. Certainly the view through the bay window and the apparition of the green flares belong to the distant summer of 1928, at Yaddo in Saratoga Springs, when the ghost of a child, the daughter of the house, who had drowned years before in the lily pond at the foot of the rose garden, invaded my chamber in the tower, shattering the casement — or so I believed. And just as certainly the vision of the bleached faces peering in at me goes even further back, to the night-terrors of my childhood in Worcester, where the wind-tossed branches of the elm scraped on the glass of the fatherless house.

Nothing that I have said is meant to suggest that a poem, any poem, is at best an inspired pastiche, reducible to the sum of its constituent elements. One has hoped against the odds that it is something more, something at once capricious, idiosyncratic, and whole; not only bits and pieces, not only parts of speech, not only artful play, but one's own signature, the occult and passionate grammar of a life.

REMEMBERING GUSTON

Of all the artists I have been close to through the years, Philip Guston was unquestionably the most daemonic. This daemon in him had an enormous appetite — for life and art and food and drink and friendship and, I mustn't forget, talk — not gossip or frivolous banter, but high talk through the night on the grand themes that agitate a serious mind, excited talk, with little pockets of moisture bubbling at the corners of his mouth. Others who drifted in and out of the room eventually collapsed or disappeared; but at dawn Philip was still in top form, replenishing his vehemence with a last or next-to-last nightcap, as we raided the refrigerator and brewed a fresh pot of coffee. That is my image of Philip from the fifties and sixties, before he turned his back on the New York art world and settled permanently with Musa in Woodstock, a move that somehow signaled for me the end of an era, the breaking-up of a world of exhilarating companionships. Things were never quite the same after that.

Volcanic is another word I think of in connection with Philip. He did not so much occupy his physical frame as seethe within it. His rage was always perilously close to the surface, ready for instantaneous eruption, attended by a darkening of his whole countenance and a creasing of his brow. On such occasions you could almost watch the horns growing out of his temples. He did not suffer fools gladly, or at all. About his work he was superlatively touchy. Once a woman, a stranger, gave him a lift from a party. As they were driving along, she made polite conversation by telling him that she preferred his older paintings to his new. "Stop the car!" Philip shouted and jumped out on the highway.

In 1976, when I was Consultant in Poetry to the Library of Congress, the Smithsonian Institution commissioned him, in collaboration with me, to design a poster celebrating the marriage of poetry and painting. The poster that he executed, in his late brutal style, incorporating some of my lines, was an extraordinary work, so powerful in fact that it succeeded in frightening the people at the Smithsonian. As part of our contract, Philip and I had agreed to conduct a public dialogue in Washington, but the event was cancelled on the eve. "Bastards!" cried Philip. "They think they can treat us like a pair of old farts!" And then, as if to compensate for our failed expectations, he made a beautiful gesture, presenting me with the original painting — oil on paper — together with a set of magnificent drawings based on other poems of mine that he favored. These are treasures.

How much Philip loved poetry! One of my most vivid recollections is of an evening when I read the poems of Hopkins aloud to him at his request, for he had never heard them spoken. There were a few other friends in the room, but what I concentrated on was his face, aglow, as I had scarcely seen it before, except when he talked of Piero della Francesca, who stood in his eyes for the incorruptible glory of art.

> My heart in hiding
> Stirred for a bird, — the achieve of, the mastery of the thing!

> Brute beauty and valour and act, oh, air, pride, plume here
> Buckle! AND the fire that breaks from thee then, a billion
> Times told lovelier, more dangerous, O my chevalier!

> No wonder of it: shéer plód makes plough down sillion
> Shine, and blue-bleak embers, ah my dear,
> Fall, gall themselves, and gash gold-vermilion.

MY MOTHER'S STORY
(Yetta Helen Dine: 1866–1952)

PREFATORY NOTE: When I was asked a few years ago to write about myself, I felt impelled to deliver a straightforward report on my origins:

It was not an auspicious beginning. A few weeks before my birth in 1905 my father, of whom I know practically nothing aside from his name, killed himself. The ostensibly prosperous dress-manufacturing business in Worcester, Massachusetts, that my parents operated was discovered to be bankrupt. My mother, not yet forty, with three children to support, opened a dry-goods shop and sewed garments in the back room. Out of pride and honor she drove herself to pay off her inheritance of debts, though she had no legal obligation to do so. She was a woman of formidable will, staunch heart, and razor-sharp intelligence, whose only school was the sweatshops of New York, to which she had come alone as a young woman from her native Lithuania. After a few years of widowhood she owned a substantial enterprise again, feeding her designs to a capacious loft humming with machines. She must have been one of the first women to run a large-scale business in this country.

My mother had little time to give to her family, and my older sisters seemed somehow detached from my secret life. When I was eight, I was presented with a stepfather, Mark Dine, a gentle and scholarly man who was no help at all to my mother in her busines, but who showed me the ways of tenderness and affection. His death six years later left me desolate. Both my sisters married and died young. My mother survived these onslaughts, as well as another bankruptcy —

precipitated by her reluctance to discharge any of her employees in a time of depression — and lived alertly to the age of eighty-six, articulate to the last on the errors of capitalism and the tragedy of existence.

The account that follows derives from notes written in longhand by my mother in 1951, when she was eighty-five. The previous year she had suffered a stroke that left her weakened but not disabled, with a mind as nimble as ever and a memory, even of old street addresses, that can only be described as extraordinary. She was accustomed to an active and productive life and bitterly resented her confinement to a nursing home in Mount Vernon, New York. On one of my visits, when she complained about the wasteful indolence of her days, I suggested that she occupy herself with putting down on paper for me the untold story of her life. This she did in the months that followed with intense concentration and excitement until she came to the year of her arrival in Worcester and her fateful marriage to Solomon Kunitz, my father — events still too painful for her to recall — after which she wrote no more.

S.K.

Without my consent I was brought into the world in the year 1866, much too early and in the wrong place as if I had any choice in the matter. It was a Godforsaken village of three hundred families in Lithuania in the province of Kovno. My name at birth was Yetta Helen Jasspon. We were one of about a hundred Jewish families in Yashwen. The rest of the population consisted of Lithuanians and Poles, with a sprinkling of Germans.

My father was a descendant of Sephardic Jews who had left Spain in the sixteenth century. He and his family were proud of their Spanish origin. In fact, their adopted surname Jasspon, in Russian "Yaspan," means "I'm Spanish." Ever since I can remember he was in poor health, as the result of an incident that happened before I was born, when he was strung from a tree by a band of Polish troopers during a pogrom and almost died of hanging before he was rescued. If my mother had not appeared on the scene, waving a letter of safe-conduct from Count Radziwill, he would surely have perished. At that time the Poles and the Russians were fighting for possession of the land. My father was caught in the middle, since he was a grain merchant, whose chief customers were army horses, regardless of their nationality. He also owned several lime-pits, which were under contract to the Russian government for use in the construction of buildings and railroads. He was a learned man, who loved to give orders, and his orders were law. We all feared our lord and master and would never dare to contradict or disobey him. He had come to Yashwen from Vilna in 1846 to marry my mother's older sister, who died six years later, leaving him one daughter. A year or so later he married my mother, who bore him five children, of whom I was the fourth.

My mother's family, named Wolpe, had lived in Yashwen for six or seven generations; she and I were both born in the same house. The Wolpes were a large clan, who had settled all over Poland and near the German border. My great-great-grandfather on my mother's side was reputed to be the wisest man of his time. He was very pious and could perform miracles. People came from miles around to receive his blessing. As for his miracles, the only one that ever convinced me was that he lived to the age of a hundred and one. My mother was good-natured, warm-hearted, and hard-working, and she was my father's slave. In those days every woman was her husband's slave.

Compared with most of the people in the village, we were relatively well-off. Our house had chimneys and was built of square-cut logs, the walls were plastered, and the floors were made of wood, not clay. The three rooms were comfortably heated by a tile stove. For cooking and baking we had a large Dutch oven, made of brick. Under the kitchen was a storage cellar for vegetables and adjoining it were several outbuildings that served as barns and warehouses for grain. We kept cows and horses, a couple of goats, and of course chickens. Why anyone bothered with chickens I don't know, for you could buy eggs then for ten kopecks a dozen. The house was full of Russian and German books. My father also had a large library of Hebrew literature, displayed on shelves where nobody could miss seeing them. The oldest of these books he treasured dearly, for they had been brought from Spain by his ancestors.

Most of the villagers, ten or twelve to a family, lived in a single room heated by a clay oven, on top of which as many as possible slept at night, while the chickens clucked underneath. Those who couldn't be accommodated on top of the stove slept on benches along the walls. Every household had a couple of spinning wheels and a hand-made loom. There was no chimney, the windows were tiny, and the single door opened into the stable. All the roofs were thatched. These people lived wretchedly, but they never complained, for they had been promised a place in heaven. The little money they earned, from their produce or livestock, went to the church or to the saloons. The five saloons in town did a thriving business.

When I was twelve years old I read Spinoza in my father's library and I lost my God. Spinoza did not deny the existence of God, but he destroyed my faith in a personal divinity. Whatever adversity befalls us is either the result of our own fault or that of others. In all the troubles I've had since my childhood I've always blamed myself for my misfortune, because I could not believe it was God's will.

It was a time when people were turning from ignorance and slavery to knowledge and freedom. A spirit of restlessness infected them. They became dissatisfied with the promise of a heaven to come and wanted to enjoy their life on earth. Books and poems suddenly appeared, calling on youth to wake up and build a better world. Everywhere young people left the towns and villages of their birth and fled to the cities in search of something, they didn't know what.

My father's health declined, and his business became less and less profitable. No business could be conducted with the government honestly. Everyone demanded bribes. At the age of fourteen I left home and went to Kovno to earn my living as a clerk in a neighborhood store. My pay was fifteen rubles a year, with room and board. I felt very happy and considered myself lucky to live in the capital, where there were streetlights, sidewalks, paved streets, a nice park where the military band played every evening, and water drawn right from a faucet in the kitchen, at the back of the store, which served as my living quarters. I worked for Miss Amsterdam, a young unmarried lady — and when I say lady I really mean it, for she took an interest in me and treated me like her own child. She was well-educated, cultured, and lovable. In spite of being a rabbi's daughter she was not religious and had radical ideas. The few people she associated with were all radicals. Tolstoy was their God. Miss Amsterdam was not only my employer, but also my teacher. I remained with her for a number of years until she sold her business and went to Saint Petersburg to live. In the meantime my father had died, and I returned home at the request of my mother, who was ill and struggling to get along by renting out part of the house. Together with my younger brother we tended a vegetable garden and kept one cow and a few chickens.

To be poor in those days was more than an inconvenience, it was also a disgrace. I hated small-town life with all its discomforts, its public bath house open once a week for women, mud more than a foot deep in rainy weather, ignorance and superstition around you, everyone watching everything you did. I decided to go to America.

I scraped together the money needed for the voyage. My mother packed my trousseau, which she had been collecting since I was three, into two large wicker baskets with strong brass locks. My trousseau consisted of a feather bed and three large pillows, some seventy pounds of pure white down and goose feathers, with every quill removed by hand; dozens of hand-knit stockings of cotton or linen, which I could never wear in this country; all sorts of pure linen sheets, pillowcases, and towels; hundreds of useless objects;

[78]

a few charms for good luck; and stacks of copper and silver household utensils passed down in the family for generations. My two baskets weighed close to three hundred pounds.

I left in August 1890, crossing the German border at night, since I had no passport, and boarded a train for Bremen. There I purchased my ticket for New York and stayed four days in a charity hotel called Emigranten Haus. On the fifth day we were put on a train bound for Antwerp, where we waited ten more days in the same sort of place. During this period agents approached us with offers of jobs. People with families were offered jobs in Fall River in the cotton mills. They were even given tickets for the boat from New York to Fall River. Men from eastern Europe, mostly Slavs, were told of the prosperity awaiting them in the Pennsylvania coal mines. Those who took the jobs were advised to keep quiet about them on arrival, since a law had just been passed forbidding contract labor.

On the Red Star liner *Rhineland* we traveled steerage, four to a windowless cubicle deep in the hold. Our main meal consisted of potatoes boiled in their skins and herring served with bread and tea, but who cared about food on our way to the Golden Land? It was a rough trip, but I proved to be a good sailor and spent most of my time on deck, meeting all the passengers and listening to their plans. The men all planned to become successful merchants, worrying more about what they would do with their fortune than how they would earn it. They had almost nothing left after paying for their passage, but hope, courage, and ambition sustained them. Single girls counted on marrying rich men, of whom there were plenty in America. I listened to all, but my own heart was heavy.

At 9:30 A.M. on September 22, 1890, we passed the Statue of Liberty and docked at Castle Garden. It happened to be my twenty-fourth anniversary, but the day I landed in America was the day of my rebirth and my real birthday. I regret that twenty-four years — the best part of a life — were wasted.

With my two wicker baskets and my bundle I passed through

the gates of Castle Garden and went out into the streets of New York in search of a new life.

I told my plight to a countryman of mine, himself a recent immigrant, who had come to meet his sister off the same boat. When she finally showed up, he volunteered to take me to a relative of his at 38 Chrystie Street on the Lower East Side, where I could spend the night. By the time we arrived, late in the afternoon, I was hot, tired, and hungry. We had to climb four flights to reach our haven, a two-room tenement at the rear, occupied by a family of five. In the long dark hall at each level were a sink and toilet, serving all four families on the floor. All the doors were open and all the neighbors were talking to one another, as they waited for their turn at the sink or to use the toilet. The lady of the house greeted me and made me feel at home. I stared out of the kitchen window at the opposite brick wall and studied the five-story-high lacework of clotheslines, which were drawn by pulleys — a real novelty to me. The display of faded bedding, infants' garments, and well-worn clothes made me think of flags of welcome. Since there was not room to spare, my wicker baskets and bundle were placed on the fire escape. Soon curious neighbors came in with all kinds of excuses to survey the new arrival. It was like a homecoming party. Everyone tried to be helpful in those days.

About seven o'clock the man of the house arrived from work, accompanied by the family boarder. As soon as my presence was hastily explained, he was as friendly as could be and wished me luck in the land of opportunity. We all sat down, together with their two lovely children, who had been playing in the street, and shared the dinner, which tasted delicious to me. From our conversation I could see that he was of the new generation that had sprung up in Russia, an intellectual. But here he had become a cap maker and worked in a sweatshop. The next morning, before I left for a room a couple of blocks away, I paid for my first meal in America — twelve cents. My new friend did not want to be paid, but I insisted, and she finally took the money. This was all her boarder paid her, and she certainly would not charge me more. I have never forgotten her.

I left to explore New York and to exchange my forty-four rubles — all my wealth — into American money. At Yarmulosky's Bank on Canal Street they gave me twenty-one dollars and some change for my good Russian rubles. I felt sad that my capital had shrunk so much and wondered how long I could live on what I had. The charge for my new room, with breakfast and dinner, was $3.50 a week — not much, but equivalent in Russian money to 7 rubles. One thing I could not understand was why so many little shops had wooden Indians standing in their doorways. Also I wondered how one man, named Ice Cream, could own so many stores. He must be very rich, I thought. When I had my first taste of ice cream a few days later, I was glad that I had not revealed my ignorance to anyone.

I did not know where to look for work. A girl I met promised to take me to the shop where she was working on men's shirts. The next morning she called for me at a quarter to seven. The shop was at 22 Bayard Street, in a tenement house, where the proprietors lived in the same room with their six or eight sewing machines. The operators were of both sexes, and the place smelled of cooking and perspiration, so mixed that I couldn't tell which was stronger. The noise was deafening, what with the clatter of the machines, the bawling of the children, and the loud singing of the operators. After looking me over, the boss said he was willing to hire me under the following terms: I would have to make a down payment of five dollars on my sewing machine, after which I would be charged three dollars a month for its use; the first three weeks I would work for nothing; then, if I proved competent, I would be paid at the rate of three dollars for a whole week's work, amounting to seventy-two hours. I surveyed the room and its inhabitants and decided not to accept this wonderful opportunity. I did not like the people who worked there, the place itself, or the conditions of employment. So I left without the job.

On lower Broadway, at Howard Street, between Broadway and Center, I saw a sign: OPERATORS ON SHIRTWAISTS WANTED. I felt a little nervous as I climbed the stairs to the second floor. The foreman asked me whether I was an experienced operator, for they did not hire inexperienced help. I assured him I was, which was not the truth. At his instructions the forelady showed me to a machine and gave me some material to work on. In my broken English I told her that I was used to operating a Singer Sewing Machine, not a Wheeler and Wilson like the one in front of me. She agreed to show me how to thread it. I began sewing straight seams, but very slowly, of course, praying that the thread would not break, for I had no confidence I could fix it. Meanwhile the forelady, who had been watching me from a distance, reported to the foreman that I had lied about my experience. When I saw him approach, my heart began to beat faster. He told me I would have to leave, for they could not bother with beginners or run the risk of having their material spoiled. When I kept repeating that I could learn, he began to grow impatient with me. Nobody was a born operator, I said; they were all beginners once. If others had learned, so could I. As for his fears about my spoiling material, I was willing to pay for any damage I did. "Look!" I said. "Here is all the money I have. Take it as a guarantee." At this moment the manufacturer's wife came over from the cutting table to see what we were arguing about. When she heard my story, she took pity on me and handed me back my money. Then she sat down beside me and gave me a few pointers about operating the machine. I worked very carefully and did not hurry, but tried to do the job well. In no time I picked up speed. My first week's pay, at piecework, was over nine dollars without overtime. Within four months I was promoted to working on samples and paid by the week — sixteen dollars, which was a small fortune. The firm's name was M. I. Nathan, The Magnet Waist Co. I stayed there until I left New York to be married in Worcester, Massachusetts.

TABLE TALK
A *Paris Review* Interview

NOTE: During the winter of 1977 my Provincetown friend and neighbor Chris Busa came to New York to talk with me, over drinks, about poetry and related matters. The full account of our conversation, consolidating two afternoons of taping, eventually appeared in the *Paris Review*, Number 83, Spring 1982. This is a somewhat abbreviated version of that text, with minor editorial changes. I am grateful to Mr. Busa and the *Paris Review* for granting permission to reprint the interview.

S.K.

INTERVIEWER

Is it an actual fact, as you indicate in "The Portrait," that your father killed himself in a public park some months before you were born?

KUNITZ

I really didn't know too much about it. It floated in the air during my childhood. I never had any specific information. I didn't know the exact details until I happened to be in Worcester a few years ago for a reading. I went over to the city hall and asked for my father's death certificate and there it was. Age thirty-nine. Death by suicide. Carbolic acid. It would have torn his guts out. Strong stuff. I'm not sure how I learned he did it in a park. Maybe my older sister told me. That scene has always haunted me. There's a reference to it in a poem called "The Hemorrhage." He becomes the fallen king, a Christ figure. My original title was "The Man in the Park."

Your father has always figured strongly in your poetry, and he continues to do so in *The Testing-Tree*. But I noticed here, for the first time, that your mother asserts a prominence.

KUNITZ

That's true. My mother has become closer to me in recent years. I understand her more than I did in the beginning. There were two strong wills in that household, hers and mine, so that our natural tensions were magnified. We held each other at a distance. She was the most competent woman I have ever known — I respected that. But it took years — after her death at eighty-six — for me to be touched by the beauty and bravery of her spirit.

INTERVIEWER

In *The Testing-Tree*, though, there isn't quite that portrait of her. She seems a woman of unforgiveness. She is "a grey eye peeping." She guards you joylessly. In "The Portrait" she refuses to forgive your father for killing himself.

KUNITZ

Well, she was unconcessive in many ways. And it's true that she refused ever to speak to me about my father. She obliterated every trace of him. In her very last years, at my request, she began writing her memoirs. It's a remarkable document, which I will someday use in one form or other. She is fresh and vital writing about her childhood in Russia. And her emigration to this country. And her work as an operator in the sweatshops of New York's Lower East Side. About everything until she moved to Worcester. Until she met my father. Then she froze, and wrote no more.

INTERVIEWER

Where in Russia did she come from?

KUNITZ

Lithuania.

[84]

Did she speak Lithuanian or Russian at home?

No. She spoke English, though she was twenty-four when she came here in 1890, with no knowledge of the language. She went to night school, read a good deal, educated herself.

Was there much discussion of Russian writers in your house, as a boy?

Not a great deal. But there was a good library. For that period and for that middle-class world, rather exceptional. There was a complete set of Tolstoy, complete Dickens, complete Shakespeare. An unabridged dictionary. A big illustrated Bible — both Testaments. A lot of history, history of all nations. The classic books. Gibbon. Goethe. Dante's *Inferno* illustrated by Gustave Doré. There was a sense of civilization there.

You say very directly in "An Old Cracked Tune" that "my mother's breast was thorny, / and father I had none." Is this comfortless situation based simply on her attitude toward your father or did it arrive out of your relationship with her?

My mother was a working woman, absent all day — in that era a rare phenomenon. She was one of the pioneer businesswomen, a dress designer and manufacturer. I was always left in the care of others and didn't have an intimate day-to-day contact with her. When she came home in the evening, she was tired and easily vexed, impatient with my moodiness. She was not one to demonstrate affection physically — in fact, I don't recall ever being kissed by her during my childhood. Yet I never doubted her fierce love for me. And pride in me for my little scholastic triumphs and early literary productions.

My favorite poem of yours is "King of the River," and I believe my reason is that the salmon, ostensibly the subject of the poem, is half fish, half Kunitz. Could we talk a little about how the poem came into being?

What triggered "King of the River," I recall, was a brief report in *Time* of some new research on the aging process of the Pacific salmon. I wrote the poem in Provincetown one fall — my favorite writing season. The very first lines came to me with their conditional syntax and suspended clauses, a winding and falling movement. The rest seemed to flow, maybe because I'm never very far from the creature world. Some of my deepest feelings have to do with plants and animals. In my bad times they've sustained me. It may be pertinent that I experienced a curious elation while confronting the unpleasant reality of being mortal, the inexorable process of my own decay. Perhaps I had managed to "distance" my fate — the salmon was doing my dying for me.

A poem has secrets that the poet knows nothing of. It takes on a life and a will of its own. It might have proceeded differently — toward catastrophe, resignation, terror, despair — and I still would have to claim it. Valéry said that poetry is a language within a language. It is also a language beyond language, a meta-medium — that is, metabolic, metaphoric, metamorphic. A poet's collected work is his book of changes. The great meditations on death have a curious exaltation. I suppose it comes from the realization, even on the threshold, that one isn't done with one's changes.

Isn't it true that a poet has preferences among his own poems in the same way that he has preferences among the poems of other poets? That specialness isn't always based on sheer quality. You yourself have defended a line from "Father and Son" that critics have complained was obscure or ugly even. If I remember, the line went: ". . . the night nailed like an orange to my brow." But you felt that nails and fruit have had a long history in your consciousness and that you didn't give a damn whether someone liked it or not. Do you have any of that obstinate fondness for this poem?

KUNITZ

Some days I have an obstinate fondness for all my poems. Other days I dislike them intensely. I'll concede that the poems of mine that stay freshest for me in the long run are the archetypal ones, of which "King of the River" is undoubtedly an example. I mean archetypal in the Jungian sense, with reference to imagery rooted in the collective unconscious. I am no longer attracted to or tempted by the sort of metaphysical abstraction that led me in my youth to write — somewhat presumptuously, it seems to me now — of daring "to vie with God for His eternity." The images I seek are those derived from bodily immersion in what Conrad called "the destructive element." That salmon battering toward the dam. . . .

INTERVIEWER

Is this a Christian God you're contending with?

KUNITZ

Call Him the God of all gods. I have no sectarian faith.

INTERVIEWER

Theodore Roethke mentions in one of his letters that "Kunitz called me the best Jewish poet in America." I was wondering what you meant by that.

KUNITZ

It sounds like me, but I don't remember the occasion. I was probably just teasing him about being guilt-ridden and full of moral imperatives. Besides, he had inherited some anti-Semitic reflexes from his Prussian ancestors.

I'm trying to find a delicate way of asking you to comment on a rather offensive characterization of you by Harold Bloom. He includes you with several poets who he feels have evaded their Jewish heritage in their poetry.

KUNITZ

Cripes!

INTERVIEWER

Insofar as your poems are morally conscious they may be construed to be Jewish. The son in "Father and Son" asks his absent father to "teach me to be kind." One great aim of your work is to discover the ethical content of your own unconscious.

KUNITZ

It's obvious that Jewish cultural aspiration and ethical doctrine entered into my bloodstream, but in practice I am an American freethinker, a damn stubborn one, and my poetry is not hyphenated. I said a few minutes ago that I had no religion, but I should have added that I have strong religious feelings. Moses and Jesus and Lao-tse have all instructed me. And the prophets as well, from Isaiah to Blake — though Blake is closer to me. I had never thought of it before, but it's true that three of the poets who most strongly influenced me — Donne, Herbert, Hopkins — happen to have been Christian churchmen.

INTERVIEWER

Bloom's point was that the Jewish poet cannot offer his wholehearted surrender to a Gentile precursor.

KUNITZ

Bloom should ask himself why all his poets are WASPs.

INTERVIEWER

In the years before 1959, when you were awarded the Pulitzer Prize, you were relatively obscure as a poet. Can I have your reasons for that?

[88]

I am not and never was a prolific or fashionable poet. For a long time I lived apart from the literary world, in rural isolation. During my middle years my poems were said to be too dark and obscure, though they seem quite intelligible now. To this day I've had very little serious critical attention. Maybe I don't know how lucky I've been!

I detect certain mannerisms of Eliot in some of the early poems.

Eliot invented a tone of voice and put his stamp on the metaphysical mode. In my generation, the next after his, one would have to be a fool not to learn something from him. But in fundamental respects I rejected what he stood for. From the beginning I was a subjective poet in contradiction to the dogma propounded by Eliot and his disciples that objectivity, impersonality, was the goal of art. Furthermore, I despised his politics. It's ironic that a generation later, when confessional poetry, so called, became the rage, I was classified as a late convert to the confessional school. That made me laugh and shudder. My struggle is to use the life in order to transcend it, to convert it into legend.

What were some of the other pressures that brought about the looser style of the poems in *The Testing-Tree?*

The language of my poetry's always been accessible, even when the syntax was complex. I've never used an esoteric vocabulary, though some of my information may have been special. I believe there is such an intrinsic relationship between form and content that the moment you start writing a poem in pentameters you tend to revert to an Elizabethan idiom. "Night Letter," for example, is rhetorically an Elizabethan poem. What strikes me, as I read and reread the poetry and prose of the Elizabethans, is that they had a longer breath unit — their language was still bubbling and rich in qualifiers, in adjectives and adverbs. The nouns and verbs of Shakespeare couldn't, by themselves, fulfill the line and give it enough richness of texture for the Renaissance taste. I acquired a taste for that kind of opulence of language, but as the years went on I began to realize that my breath units didn't require so long a line. By my middle period I was mainly working with tetrameters, which eliminated at least one adjective from every line. In my current phase I've stripped that down still more. I want the energy to be concentrated in my nouns and verbs, and I write mostly in trimeters, since my natural span of breath seems to be three beats. It seems to me so natural now that I scarcely ever feel the need for a longer line. Sometimes I keep a little clock going when people talk to me and I notice they too are speaking in trimeters. Back in the Elizabethan Age I'd have heard pentameters.

INTERVIEWER

Does the increased accessibility of the poems in *The Testing-Tree* indicate a significant change in your aesthetic?

KUNITZ

At my age, after you're done — or ruefully think you're done — with the nagging anxieties and complications of your youth, what is there left for you to confront but the great simplicities? I never tire of bird-song and sky and weather. I want to write poems that are natural, luminous, deep, spare. I dream of an art so transparent that you can look through and see the world.

INTERVIEWER

Occasionally a poem of yours — "The War Against the Trees" is an example — will sound mock heroic on the page, and I am surprised that the tone in which I've heard you read it is not at all mock heroic.

KUNITZ

Irony is one of the ingredients there — but I shouldn't call it mock heroic.

Take a line like this: ". . . the bulldozers, drunk with gasoline, / Tested the virtue of the soil." Or: "All day the hireling engines charged the trees . . . forcing the giants to their knees." It's the magnification of the event and the personification of the bulldozers and the trees.

Well, I suppose that for me the rape of nature is an event of a certain magnitude. My feeling for the land is more than an abstraction. I've always been mad about gardening, and used to think, when I was struggling to survive, that I could end my days quite happily working as a gardener on some big estate. In Provincetown I tend my terraces flowering on the bay. I'm out there grubbing every summer morning. The man in one of my poems who "carries a bag of earth on his back" must be my double.

One doesn't think of you as a pastoral poet, but you draw a good deal of your sustenance from the natural world. For most of your adult life you've chosen to live in the country.

With the first five hundred dollars I saved after coming to New York I bought a hundred-acre farm on Wormwood Hill in Mansfield Center, Connecticut, and moved there with my first wife. That was in 1930. I loved the woods and fields and the grand old eighteenth-century house, with its gambrel roof. But we were poor, and living conditions were primitive, without electricity or central heating or even running water. Eventually I made the improvements that the house required — mostly with my own hands — but I couldn't save the marriage. Later, for the span of my second marriage, I lived in Bucks County, Pennsylvania — beautiful country. That's the locale of "River Road." I've always needed space around me, a piece of ground to cultivate, and the feel of living creatures. I'm never bored in the country. Very few of my poems deal with urban situations.

What about the need for friendship and literary stimulation?

I didn't realize what I was missing until one evening Ted Roethke drove down to New Hope from Lafayette and knocked at my door, unannounced, with a copy of *Intellectual Things* in his hand. It astonished me that this big, shambling stranger knew my poems by heart.

Roethke at this time had published only a few poems?

He had published practically nothing, but was working on the poems that eventually became *Open House*. That was a saving relationship for both of us. I sensed he needed me even more than I needed him.

You were both lonely. But he sought somebody out.

He was much more aggressive than I, more socially ambitious, and he soon had a world of literary friendships, of which I would hear when he came to see me. He would tell me about Louise Bogan and Léonie Adams and Rolfe Humphries and, a bit later, Auden and all the others that he sought out and gathered to him. But he did not bring us together. His policy was to keep his friends apart.

Were you a loner on some principle or were you naturally shy?

As a young man I was preternaturally shy. For years it was difficult for me to reach out to others. I'd lived such an inward life for so long. I think I'm more open with people now.

In your early poems there are fairly frequent references to your youth as being a period of despair, as if you resented it. In one you say, ". . . innocence betrayed me in a room of mocking elders."

KUNITZ

I've been through many dark nights, but the guilts I've expressed aren't meant to be interpreted confessionally. Somebody once asked me, quite bluntly, what it was I felt so guilty about. I replied, "For being fallible and mortal." Does that make me sound terribly glum? Believe me, I've had my share of joys. And I'm still ready for more.

INTERVIEWER

You had an unhappy period in the army during World War II. What were the circumstances?

KUNITZ

Briefly, I was drafted, just short of my thirty-eighth birthday, as a non-affiliated pacifist, with moral scruples against bearing arms. My understanding with the draft board was that I would be assigned to a service unit, such as the Medical Corps. Instead the papers on my status got lost or were never delivered, and I was shuttled for three years from camp to camp, doing KP duty most of the time or digging latrines. A combination of pneumonia, scarlet fever, and just downright humiliation almost did me in. While I was still in uniform, *Passport to the War,* my bleakest book, was published, but I was scarcely aware of the event. It seemed to sink without a trace.

INTERVIEWER

In the period before you went into the army, what magazines were you publishing in?

KUNITZ

I was publishing very little then. Witty, elegant, Audenesque poems were in demand then, not mine. I was lucky to get my book published at all. Practically every major publishing firm rejected it before Holt took it. I had the same unflattering experience with my *Selected Poems,* fourteen years later, before Atlantic accepted them.

INTERVIEWER

Aside from Roethke, did you have any staunch supporters?

KUNITZ

I had more than I knew, but no lines of communication between us. Imagine my surprise to learn, on my discharge from the army in '45, that I had been awarded a Guggenheim fellowship, for which I had never applied. When I inquired how it could have happened, I was told that Marianne Moore, whom I wasn't to meet until years later, had been my intercessor.

INTERVIEWER

Your earlier poems have been accused — I should say that is the right word — of being overly intellectual . . .

KUNITZ

(laughs) . . . which is nonsense.

INTERVIEWER

But when one dwells on the paradox that such work as you have produced is urbane only in its complexity, not in its concerns, then one begins to see that there is something real in your choice to live apart from the city. Perhaps there is something about much thought, small conversation, and the endless blue of country skies that stunts the smart aleck and develops one's mystical sense, as if one is left without a language adequate for wonder. In the language that one does find, there is both great strain and mystical attainment.

KUNITZ

One of my primary convictions is that I am not a reasonable poet.

One of your poems — "The Science of the Night" — has a passage: "We are not souls but systems, and we move in clouds of our unknowing." Is that a direct reference to the text by the medieval religious mystic?

Yes. *The Cloud of Unknowing* — haunting phrase. But, sure, I think that what we strive for is to move from the world of our immediate knowing, our limited range of information, into the unknown. My poems don't come easy — I have to fight for them. In my struggle I have the sense of swimming underwater toward some kind of light and open air that will be saving. Redemption is a theme that concerns me. We have to learn how to live with our frailties. The best people I know are inadequate and unashamed.

Can you say something about how you manage to find "the language that saves"?

The poem in the head is always perfect. Resistance starts when you try to convert it into language. Language itself is a kind of resistance to the pure flow of self. The solution is to become one's language. You cannot write a poem until you hit upon its rhythm. That rhythm not only belongs to the subject matter, it belongs to your interior world, and the moment they hook up there's a quantum leap of energy. You can ride on that rhythm, it will carry you somewhere strange. The next morning you look at the page and wonder how it all happened. You have to triumph over all your diurnal glibness and cheapness and defensiveness.

One of my ideas about your poetry is that there are two voices, arguing with each other. One is the varied voice of personality, the voice that speaks in the context of a dramatic situation. The other is an internal voice, the voice that's rhythm. It governs a poem's movement the way the waves govern the movement of a boat — seldom do the two want to go in the same direction.

KUNITZ

The struggle is between incantation and sense. There's always a song lying under the surface of these poems. It's an incantation that wants to take over — it really doesn't need a language — all it needs is sounds. The sense has to struggle to assert itself, to mount the rhythm and become inseparable from it.

INTERVIEWER

Would you say that rhythm is feeling, in and of itself?

KUNITZ

Rhythm to me, I suppose, is essentially what Hopkins called the taste of self. I taste myself as rhythm.

INTERVIEWER

How wide a variety of rhythms do you feel?

KUNITZ

The psyche has one central rhythm — capable, of course, of variations, as in music. You must seek your central rhythm in order to find out who you are.

INTERVIEWER

So you would agree you could say about music that Bach's central rhythm is devotional and Mozart's is gay, sunny, and exuberant. How would you define your own rhythm in these terms?

KUNITZ

Mine, I think, is essentially dark and grieving — elegiac. Sometimes I counterpoint it, but the ground melody is what I mostly hear.

With respect to rhythm, could you discuss your term "functional stressing"?

KUNITZ

Functional stressing is simply my way of coping with the problem of writing a musical line that isn't dependent on the convention of alternating slack and stressed syllables. What I usually hear these days is a line with three strong stresses in it — that's my basic measure. I don't make a point of counting stresses — the process is largely unconscious, determined by my ear. A line can have any number of syllables, and sometimes it will add or eliminate a stress. Rhythm depends on a degree of regularity, but the imagination requires an illusion of freedom. The system of stresses is the organizing principle of a poem. I tend to dwell on long vowels and to play them against the consonants; and I love to modulate the flow of a poem, to change the pace, so that it quickens and then slows, becomes alternately fluid and clotted. The language of a poem must do more than convey experience: it must embody it.

INTERVIEWER

Is this what you look for in the poems of others, that feeling of there it "happened" to him, that feeling of oneness with his subject? Take a writer like D. H. Lawrence, who's utterly unlike you.

KUNITZ

Nevertheless, he's a poet I admire. I think of "The Snake" or, better still, "The Ship of Death" — his ecstatic funeral song. He's a dying man, sailing out toward the unknown — a rocking, redundant movement — and you're on board with him, sharing his destiny, a passenger on the same ship, which is so real you feel the flow of the sunset and the coming of the night.

INTERVIEWER

And that transcends any literary consideration?

It transcends it. You mustn't let the aesthetic of a period determine for you what's good or bad in poetry.

That's why it must be so annoying for you to have critics praise you for your skillful craft.

Oh, I hate that. I take it as a put-down. Unless craft is second nature, it means nothing. Craft can point the way, it can hone an instrument to a fine cutting edge, but it's not to be confused with an art of transformation, that magical performance.

Frost talks about the poet, or himself rather, as a performer, as an athlete is a performer. In what sense do you mean that writing is a performance?

A trapeze artist on his high wire is performing and defying death at the same time. He's doing more than showing off his skill; he's using his skill to stay alive. Art demands that sense of risk, of danger. But few artists in any period risk their lives. The truth is they're not on a high enough wire. This makes me think of an incident in my childhood. In the woods behind our house in Worcester was an abandoned quarry — you'll find mention of it in "The Testing-Tree." This deep-cut quarry had a sheer granite face. I visited it almost every day, alone in the woods, and in my magic Keds I'd try to climb it, till the height made me dizzy. I was always testing myself. There was nobody to watch me. I was testing myself to see how high I could go. There was very little ledge, almost nothing to hold on to. Occasionally I'd find a plant or a few blades of tough grass in the crevices, but the surface was almost vertical, with only the most precarious toehold. One day I was out there and I climbed — oh, it was a triumph! — almost to the top. And then I couldn't get down. I couldn't go up or down. I just clung there that whole afternoon and through the long night. Next morning the police and fire department found me. They put up a ladder and brought me down. I must say my mother didn't appreciate that I was inventing a metaphor for poetry.

INTERVIEWER

In "The Testing-Tree," when you threw the three stones against the oak, you don't mention how many hit. If you hit once, it was for love; twice, and you would be a poet; three times, and you would live forever.

KUNITZ

I got awfully efficient. In the end I almost never missed. I've always excelled at hand-and-eye coordination, any sort of ball game. That makes me think of a game I used to play with Roethke. I put a little wastebasket at one end of the room, and then we'd try to pitch tennis balls into it from the opposite corner. Each successful pitch was worth a dime. If I made ten shots in a row and he made three, he owed me seventy cents. Well, I was really phenomenal at this, and I made a small fortune from Roethke. In fact, he refused to play with me anymore because he said I was practicing during his absence. It's true enough. Sometimes I still play that game against myself.

INTERVIEWER

How did you get involved with teaching?

KUNITZ

When I was in the service I received a letter from Lewis Webster Jones, the president of Bennington, offering me a teaching job when I got out of the army. I was staggered. I had never taught before. I'd been free-lancing and editing for the H. W. Wilson Company, but I hadn't taught at all and I couldn't understand why I was being asked to come and teach at Bennington. It turned out that Roethke, who had been teaching there, had had a violent breakdown and had locked himself into his cottage, threatening anybody who came near him, especially the president. He was finally induced to carry on a conversation. He said he knew the jig was up — he'd have to leave. But he'd come out and be peaceful on one condition — that they invite me to take his place.

Did you look forward to this?

I'd always been hungry to teach, though I thought I never would after my initial rejection at Harvard.

Could you go into that?

At Harvard I stayed on for my Master's with the thought of becoming a member of the faculty. It seemed to me a not unreasonable expectation, since I had graduated *summa cum laude* and won most of the important prizes, including the Garrison Medal for Poetry. When I inquired about it, the word came back from the English faculty that I couldn't hope to teach there because "Anglo-Saxons would resent being taught English by a Jew." I was humiliated and enraged. Even half a century later I have no great feeling of warmth for my alma mater. Of course that was in the dark ages of the American academy. A few years after I left, Jews were no longer considered to be pariahs. From this vantage point I'm glad I didn't stay and become an academician. All those years of struggle taught me a great deal about the vicissitudes of life. My scrambling for survival kept me from being insulated from common experience. It certainly fed my political passions.

What did you do after you left Harvard?

I went back to Worcester and became a staff reporter on the *Worcester Telegram*. I had been a summer reporter on the *Telegram* since my sophomore year, when I wrote an impertinent letter to the editor, saying that I thought the paper could use somebody who knew how to write. As proof of my literary prowess, I enclosed an impressionistic panegyric on James Joyce — this was in 1923. In a few days, much to my amazement, I received a letter from Captain Roland Andrews, editor in chief, saying that by God I *could* write and a job was mine for the asking. As a full-time member of the staff I became assistant Sunday editor and wrote a literary column and did some features. Then I was assigned to the Sacco-Vanzetti case. I soon saw that a terrible injustice was being perpetrated. My particular assignment was to cover the judge, Judge Webster Thayer, a mean little frightened man who hated the guts of these "anarchistic bastards." He could not conceivably give them a fair trial. I was so vehement about this miscarriage of justice, so filled with it, that around the newspaper office they used to call me "Sacco." After the executions, I became obsessed with the notion that Vanzetti's eloquent letters should be published and received permission to see what I could do about it. I gave up my job on the *Telegram* and went to New York alone. I had nothing, no money, no friends. I made the rounds of the publishing houses, but nobody would touch the book. The whole country was in the grip of one of its periodic Red scares. I was virtually penniless by the time I landed a job with the H. W. Wilson Company.

INTERVIEWER

You quit your job with the *Worcester Telegram* expressly to find publication for the letters?

KUNITZ

I sensed it was time for me to leave. Curiously, I was twenty-three when I came to New York, about the same age as my mother when she landed at the immigrant station on Castle Garden.

Your career seems larger at both ends. You first published when you were quite young and now, as you have put it, you're threatening to become prolific.

KUNITZ

I like the verb "threatening."

INTERVIEWER

What sort of function or role are you trying to accomplish in your own criticism?

KUNITZ

I'm not programmatic. I suppose I try to establish the connections between language and action, aesthetics and moral values, the individual and society.

INTERVIEWER

Your pieces on other poets are invariably sympathetic at heart.

KUNITZ

I've made a point of not writing about poets with whom I am not sympathetic. There's plenty of negativism around about poets. I don't feel any need to contribute more. Of course I recognize differences. For example, my essay on Robinson Jeffers attacks his political insensibility about Hitler, but at the same time it is written with true respect for his achievement as a poet. If you understand a poet's key images, you have a clue to the understanding of his whole work. I wish criticism would spend more time in the intimate pursuit of those central images. That's a more productive concern than ratings and influences.

INTERVIEWER

What is the origin of your early imagery of spikes and cones and spheres?

I don't know. It could be religious, or cubistic, or scientific. I haven't mentioned that I had an apprenticeship with Alfred North Whitehead during my last year at Harvard. He was giving an advanced course in the nature of the physical universe. I didn't have the prerequisites, but I wanted very much to be one of the handful permitted to study with him. I went to see Whitehead. He asked me why I wanted to be in his group. I said, "I'll give you two reasons. I admire you extravagantly and I hope to be a poet." He said, "You're in." I learned a lot from him.

You also met the "Moon Man" in Worcester?

Dr. Robert H. Goddard. Yes. This was in the spring of 1926 while I was on the *Telegram*. One day the city editor said to me, "There's a crazy man in town playing around with rockets. Why don't you go over and see him?" So I went over to Clark University, where Goddard was professor of physics. I may have been the first person ever to interview him. This was shortly after he had made the great experiment outside the city limits of Worcester — in an open field in Auburn he had fired the first liquid-fueled rocket. He told me about this with quiet intensity. I said, "How high did it go?" And he said, "One hundred eighty-four feet in two point five seconds." "Is that all?" I said. His voice turned a little shrill. "Young man, don't you see? It's all solved! We'll make it to the moon! Because the principle is right, don't you see, don't you see?" He went to his blackboard. A little man, very professorial looking, completely obsessed with his calculations and diagrams. I have an unpublished poem about this encounter. He made me feel somehow connected with him, as though both of us were shooting for the moon, in different ways.

His story was your story?

I suppose I made it mine. That's the way with the imagination.

Not many poets writing during the early years of your career were attracted to science?

And no wonder. After a quarter of a century I still have to explain to audiences what I am doing with the metaphor of the red shift in "The Science of the Night." Such terminology ought to be just as common knowledge as the myths were in Ancient Greece. The vocabulary of modern science is fascinating — I read everything I can find about pulsars and black holes and charm and quarks — but, by and large, the vocabulary remains exclusive and specialized. The more we know about the universe, the less understandable it becomes. The classic world had more reality than ours. At least it thought it understood what reality was. In 1948, I recall, Niels Bohr visited Bennington and drew a neat picture of neutrons and protons on the blackboard. In the question period that followed I asked him, "Is this really the structure of the atom, or is it your metaphor for the present state of our information about it?" He preferred then not to accept that distinction. Today a diagram of the atom would look vastly different, more complicated, and I would not need to repeat the question.

Scientists think their metaphors are not heuristic.

The popular impression is that their metaphors are real and the poet's metaphors are unreal.

Why do you suppose the metaphors of scientists are taken with much more seriousness than those of poets?

Because we live in a pragmatic society, and the effects of science are evident, whereas the consequences of poetry are invisible. How many truly believe that if poetry were to be suppressed, the light of our civilization would go out?

If there are few serious readers of poetry, how is its light disseminated?

Largely it's disseminated among the young. A sizable fraction of the youth in our universities read poetry, hear poets and are excited by them. Any poet who travels across the country knows this to be true. Many of these students will go out into the world and never read another book of poems, but if only a fraction of them retain their interest, it will be a significant change for the better. It occurs to me that, though poets don't have a large readership, their product in diluted form comes down to the mass population — in popular music, popular song, in all the areas of commercialized art. Popular art in this country today is a reduced, somewhat degraded form of high art, in contrast to other epochs, when popular art fed high art. Writers of the ballads inspired the poets of the Romantic movement. Nursery rhymes entered into the imagination of the poets in all centuries. Now we are getting the reverse process — high art, in its diluted state, touches everybody. Bob Dylan couldn't have existed if Dylan Thomas hadn't existed before him.

Since the media occupy a paradoxical relationship to art as a diluter, but also as a disseminator, are they an ally of art?

They could be, but they aren't. Yet every once in a while something comes along to remind you of possibilities. Haley's *Roots* on

TV, for example, which stirred a nation's conscience — at least for a few nights. It gave white masters an opportunity to redeem themselves through guilt. Incidentally, I was in Ghana and Senegal last spring. The curious thing that struck me was that young African poets are trying to forget their tribal and colonial past. The main collective effort is to move into high technology and to overleap centuries of industrial backwardness. The poets want to jump smack into the Western world and write like Westerners. They study and imitate us. One young Ghanaian told me he felt guilty about not writing in his tribal language, but he scarcely knew it and it was too difficult to master for literary purposes. In our culture, we have a counter-phenomenon. Our poets are trying to rediscover our tribal past, the bonds that hold us together. The search back into the roots of our common life is an archetypal journey. We have to go back and reconstruct the foundation myths, so they will live again for us. Poetry is tied to memory. As we grow older, our childhood returns to us out of the mists. I may be mistaken, but my impression is that early in the century — I'm speaking in general terms — a child had fewer advantages, but he was more innocent, more hopeful, more ambitious than his grandchildren today. We really believed then that society was on our side.

INTERVIEWER

You've lived most of your life outside the poetry establishment. Do you consider yourself to be a part of it now? Has your attitude toward it changed?

KUNITZ

I wish I knew what the poetry establishment is. It's curious that nobody speaks of the fiction establishment. Poets don't get their rewards in the marketplace, so maybe they tend to take honors and prizes and the illusion of power much too seriously. There's a heavy accumulation of bile in that famous Pierian spring. Some poets seem to think they have to kill off their predecessors in order to make room for themselves. If you live long enough and receive a bit of recognition, you're bound to become a target. The only advantage of celebrity I can think of is that it puts one in a position to be of help to others. The phrase "community of poets" still has a sweet ring to me.

For sheer good company, you seem to prefer painters to poets.

I count myself lucky to be married into their world. I envy them because there is so much physical satisfaction in the actual work of painting and sculpture. I'm a physical being and resent this sedentary business of sitting at one's desk and moving only one's wrists. I pace, I speak my poems, I get very kinetic when I'm working. Besides, I love the social and gregarious nature of painters. Poets tend to be nervous and competitive and introverted. My image of discomfort is three poets together in a room. My painter friends — among them Kline and De Kooning and Rothko and Guston and Motherwell — were enacting an art of gesture to which I responded. When I insist on poetry as a kind of action, I'm thinking very much in these terms — every achieved metaphor in a poem is a gesture of sorts, the equivalent of the slashing of a stroke on canvas.

You have produced some sculpture — wire sculpture and assemblages.

Sometimes I feel I'm a sculptor *manqué*. I love working with my hands. In my garden, my woodworking. My hands want to make forms. Though my poems often deal with the time sense, I'm inclined to translate that into metaphors of space. I like to define my perimeters. I want to know where a poem is happening, its ground, its footing, how much room I have to move in.

You organize a poem spatially?

It's one of the ways a poem of mine gets organized. I follow the track of the eye — it's a track through space.

The Fine Arts Work Center in Provincetown, which you helped start, would seem to be a reflection of your concern with making a community of artists and writers.

Art withers without fellowship. I recall how grievously I missed the sense of a community in my own youth. In a typical American city or town poets are strangers. If our society provided a more satisfying cultural climate, a more spontaneous and generous environment, we shouldn't need to install specialized writing workshops in the universities or endow places like Yaddo or Mac-Dowell or Provincetown. In Provincetown we invite a number of young writers and visual artists from all parts of the country to live at the Center for an extended period, working freely in association. Our policy is not to impose a pattern on them, but to let them create their own. In practice, instead of becoming competitive, they soon want to talk to one another about their work problems, they begin to share their manuscripts and paintings, they arrange their own group sessions, they meet visiting writers and artists and consult with them, if they are so inclined. Most who come for the seven-month term are loath to leave. Many of them stay on as residents of the town.

Can you comment on the quality of the work of young poets?

I hate to generalize, but I'll make a stab at offering a few broad conclusions. My first and main observation is that no earlier generation has written so well, or in such numbers. But it's a generation without masters: dozens of poets are writing at the same level of accomplishment. My explanation is that what we're experiencing is the democratization of genius. It's also clear that few poets have much of anything to say. Practically the only exceptions are the liberated women, who have the authentic passion of a cause. It's no accident that my first five Yale selections were men, my last three female. Another point is that few young poets have mastered traditional prosody. The result is that they don't really know how to make language sing or move for them. There's a modicum of music in most of what's being written today. They're not testing their poems against the ear. They're writing for the page, and the page, let me tell you, is a cold bed.

Among your recent work, "Three Floors" stands out for its musical effects.

Studs Terkel, who interviewed me last fall in Chicago, told me it was one of his favorites. He had me read it while someone played *Warum* in the background — on tape, of course. A little corny, perhaps, but it was quite moving to hear that music, which I hadn't really heard since my childhood. I realized that I had actually written the poem to that melody. The poem goes back to more formal patterns. It's the only rhymed stanzaic poem in *The Testing-Tree*. And not because I planned it that way, but simply because it came to me that way. It would have been a lie to force it into a different mode. You have to trust the way a poem comes to you. I don't expect it to happen, but I don't negate the possibility of my returning to a more formal verse tradition.

Literary tradition has accumulated suspicions about the sincerity of any poet's feelings toward conventional subjects. There are certain poems of yours that seem oblivious to this. A poem like "Robin Redbreast" — until its ending — seems to strain sentimentally after the large problem of being a little bird, though its end is so powerful — when the robin is picked up, the poet sees the blue sky through a bullet hole in his head — that I am ashamed of my reaction to the earlier part of the poem.

KUNITZ

Maybe you're confusing pathos with sentimentality. My reverence for the chain of being is equivalent to a religious conviction. I don't apologize for my strong feelings about birds and beasts. Was Blake being sentimental when he wrote, "A robin redbreast in a cage / Puts all Heaven in a rage," or "A dog starv'd at his master's gate / Predicts the ruin of the state"?

INTERVIEWER

Often your poems deal with dreams.

KUNITZ

Often a poem *is* a dream, but I don't necessarily say it is.

INTERVIEWER

Are there any specific poems that come to mind?

KUNITZ

The one that first occurs to me is "Open the Gates." It begins with a vision of the city of the burning cloud. Like Sodom and Gomorrah — cities of the plain. Those images of dragging my life behind me and knocking on the door and the rest of it are straight out of dream. I woke at the moment of revelation, just when the gates were opening. Another source of that poem my be the Doré illustrations to Dante's *Inferno,* one of the magic books of my childhood. My images usually have an experiential root. In "The Testing-Tree" the image of my mother in the last section, the dream passage, goes back to a conversation with her in her eighties. She told me she had a proposal of marriage from a man of about the same age. He thought they should live out their lives together and

[110]

take her off my hands; it was a practical thing. I asked her: "Do you really care for him?" She shook her head. "You know there are only two old men I have any use for. One's Bernard Shaw and the other is Bertrand Russell." She meant that. Another image in the same section is of a sputtering Model A that "unfurled a highway behind / where the tanks maneuver, / revolving their turrets." In '45, after my discharge from the army, I drove a Model A cross-country, stopping on the way at a little oasis in the middle of the desert called Silver Springs. A few days later I pushed on to the West Coast. Several years later I drove back from the University of Washington, where I'd been visiting poet. I took the route through Death Valley into Nevada to see my oasis. When I approached, armed guards appeared from every side and ordered me away. It turned out that the place was now Yucca Flats, the testing ground of the atom bomb. This is all curiously in the background of the poem, somewhat mysteriously translated. And the lines about "in a murderous time": I wrote those lines the night that Martin Luther King was assassinated. I had been working on the poem for weeks, but couldn't get the ending right. I was visiting Yale at that time, reading manuscripts for the Yale Series, and staying with R.W.B. Lewis, an old friend of mine. We were listening to the radio when we heard about the assassination of King, with whom I had been associated, raising money for the civil rights movement. Suddenly, as I sat listening to the announcement, the lines I needed came to me.

INTERVIEWER

What is the source for the imagery of depreciation toward the end of this poem, such as the "cardboard doorway"?

KUNITZ

I see a movie set, furnished with memories like studio props. Doorways figure largely throughout the poem — entrances into my past, into the woods, into truth itself. I had recently gone back to Worcester to receive an honorary degree from Clark University

and had asked to be taken to the scenes of my childhood. The net-
tled field had changed into a housing development, the path into
the woods had become an express highway, and the woods them-
selves were gone. That's where the poem began, with the thought
that reality itself is dissolving all around us.

INTERVIEWER

You indicate that with images pasted together like a collage?

KUNITZ

A montage, I would say.

INTERVIEWER

Can you say something about the arrangement of the lines for
this poem?

KUNITZ

I started working with flush margins, and had difficulty achiev-
ing any sort of linear tension. Furthermore, I found the look of
the page uninteresting, that long poem with all those short lines.
I didn't develop a triadic sense until I began tinkering with the lines,
as I often do at the beginning of a poem, trying to find the formal
structure. The moment I hit on the tercets, the poem began to
move.

INTERVIEWER

I am impressed by your capacity to break the tone abruptly or
to shift the voice in a poem. Sometimes it is only for a line, but
these outbreaks seem to have an idiosyncratic dramatic function.

KUNITZ

It's something I may have learned from working with dramatic
monologues. In an extended passage I sense the need for an inter-
ruption of the speech-flow, another kind of voice breaking into
the poem and altering its course. I recall one occasion when I was
hunting for a phrase to do just that, so that I could push the poem

one step further, beyond its natural climax. My inability to achieve the right tone infuriated me. I must have tried thirty different versions, none of which worked. I was ready to beat my head on the wall when I heard myself saying, "Let be! Let be!" And there it was, simple and perfect — I had my line. If you have a dialectical mind like mine and if a poem of yours is moving more or less compulsively toward its destination, you feel the need of a pistol shot to stop the action, so that it may resume on another track, in a different mood or tempo. One of the reasons I write poems is that they make revelation possible. I sometimes think I ought to spend the rest of my life writing a single poem whose action reaches an epiphany only at the point of exhaustion, in the combustion of the whole life, and continues and renews, until it blows away like a puff of milkweed. Anybody who remains a poet throughout a lifetime, who is still a poet let us say at sixty, has a terrible will to survive. He has already died a million times and at a certain age he faces this imperative need to be reborn. All the phenomena of his life, all the memories, all the stuff that makes him feel himself, is rematerialized and reblended. He's capable of perpetuation, he turns up again in new shapes. Any poem he writes could be a hundred poems. He could take a poem written at twenty or thirty and re-experience it and come out again with something absolutely different and probably richer. He can't excuse himself by saying he has written everything he has to write. That's a damn lie. He's swamped with material, it's overwhelming.

INTERVIEWER

What are your thoughts on the way you end a poem?

KUNITZ

I think of a beginning, a middle, and an end. I don't believe in open form. A poem may be open, but then it doesn't have form. Merely to stop a poem is not to end it. I don't want to suggest that I believe in neat little resolutions. To put a logical cap on a poem is to suffocate its original impulse. Just as the truly great piece of architecture moves beyond itself into its environment, into the landscape and the sky, so the kind of poetic closure that interests me bleeds out of its ending into the whole universe of feeling and thought. I like an ending that's both a door and a window.

INTERVIEWER

Your poems are packed; they have a weight. To me, it is a question of scale.

KUNITZ

Thanks. I've heard the opposite reaction, that my poems are too heavy. One critic wrote quite recently that my poems sounded as though they had been translated from the Hungarian. I don't know why, but somehow that made me feel quite light-hearted.

INTERVIEWER

Most of your poems are written in a high style.

KUNITZ

That used to be truer than it is today. I've tried to squeeze the water out of my poems.

INTERVIEWER

Mostly in your earlier poetry you have a stylistic habit of animating abstractions by hinging them to metaphors, as in the "bone of mercy" or the "lintel of my brain."

KUNITZ

There's some confusion about this type of prepositional construction. When it has weak specification, when it incorporates a loose abstraction, it is a stylistic vice, and I've grown increasingly wary of it. I resist phrases like "stars of glory." But when I say "the broad lintel of his brain," I am perceiving the brain as a house. The brain is not, in this usage, an abstraction. It's just as real as the lintel. Pound was the first, I think, to define this particular stylistic vice, and modern criticism has blindly followed suit, without bothering to make the necessary discriminations. In any event, I don't accept arbitrary rules about poetry. Do you want to try me with another example?

Take a phrase like "the calcium snows of sleep."

I like it, though I'm not the one who should be saying so. It's fresh and it happens to be true, scientifically true. During sleep the brain deposits calcium at a faster rate than when it's conscious. Besides, the "snows of sleep" have nothing in common with the "stars of glory." The construction is legitimately possessive, analogous to the "snows of the Russian plains." Sleep is where the snow is falling.

Do you have a reading knowledge of Russian?

I've described the method of these translations in the introduction to the Akhmatova volume. If I didn't have someone to help me with the Russian text, I would certainly be lost. I've worked mostly with Max Hayward. I not only want a word-by-word translation, in the exact word order, but any kind of gloss that would be helpful to me, such as the meanings of a word's roots. The root sense of a word may supplement, or even contradict, its current usage. Etymology is one of my passions. I like to use a word in a poem with its whole history dragging like a chain behind it. And then we go over the sound. We read the poems aloud. I translate only when I feel I have some affinity with the poet. Even with respect to a poet I don't feel particularly close to — Yevtushenko, for example — when I was asked to translate some of his poems, I fastened on to some of his early lyrics, which are among the best poems he's written.

[115]

What is the affinity you feel with Voznesensky?

It was Voznesensky who got me started with the Russians. Andrei came to this country in the sixties and we met and had a good feeling about each other. How can I explain these things? He wanted me to translate him and I felt I could do it — again, selecting the poems that I wanted to translate. I enjoyed doing it, and I learned something too. Every poet I've ever translated has taught me something. One of the perils of poetry is to be trapped in the skin of your own imagination and to remain there all your life. Translation lets you crack your own skin and enter the skin of another. You identify with somebody else's imagination and rhythm, and that makes it possible for you to become other. It's an opening toward transformation and renewal. I wish I could translate from all the languages. If I could live forever, I'd do that.

Many of the Russian poets you've known personally. Do you feel different about Baudelaire, whom you know only through his work?

I know Baudelaire too — he was dealing with exactly the kind of issues that concern me. Problems of good and evil, the sexual drama. As a young man I was attracted to the violence of his inner life, the force of his rhetoric, and the hard structure of his poems, the way they build and make such a solidity of thought and image and feeling. In a poem like "Rover" I am very aware of my debt to him. The life of a poet is crystallized in his work, that's how you know him. Akhmatova I never met. She died in '66 and I never encountered her, but she's an old friend of mine in spirit. She taught me something, taught me the possibility of dealing quite directly with the most painful experiences.

You are referring to the execution of her husband and the imprisonment of her son, as well as the government repression of her poetry?

Requiem 1935–40 is a good example. The background of the poem was excruciating, and yet out of it she made a poem that is personal at its immediate level but universal in its ultimate form. It transcends the personal by viewing the historic occasion through the lens of individual suffering. Nothing is diminished in her poems: all her adversities and humiliations. She wrote with such burning and scrupulous intensity that she became part of the historic process itself — its conscience and its voice.

Do you envy the disasters of other poets, even if those disasters lack the historical dimension of Akhmatova's?

Sufficient unto each poet are his own disasters! The victims of history have a certain grandeur. One saves one's tears for those who fall victim to themselves. Their cries lacerate us. I'm thinking of Berryman, Sexton, Plath. . . . Perhaps it is in the nature of our age to be most moved by poems born of weakness rather than of strength. All the same, I yearn for an art capable of overriding the shames, the betrayals, the lies; capable of building something shining and great out of the ruins. The poets that seem most symptomatic of the modern world are poets without what Keats called Negative Capability. They do not flow into others. The flow of their pity is inward rather than outward. They are self-immersed and self-destroying. And when they kill themselves, we love them most. That says something about our age.

The tragic sense no longer seems pertinent to our lives.

The tragic sense cannot exist without tradition and structure, the communal bond. The big machines of industry and state are unaffected by our little fates. All the aggrandizement of the ego in the modern world seems a rather frivolous enterprise, unattached to anything larger than itself. Number 85374 on the assembly line may have a life important to himself and his family, but when he reaches sixty-five and it forced out of the line, another number steps in and takes his place — and it doesn't make any difference. The artist in the modern world is probably the only person, with a handful of exceptions, who keeps alive that sense of the sharing of his life with others. When he watches that leaf fall, it's falling for you. Or that sparrow . . .

INTERVIEWER

The most difficult thing is that the adversary does not inspire confrontation. Evil has lost its cape and sharp horns. Hitler was evil but he was not a satanic figure.

KUNITZ

The opportunity for confrontation with evil was greater in an earlier age. It becomes more and more difficult to intercede in behalf of one's own fate. The overwhelming technological superiority of the military apparatus protects the tyrant, as an emblem of evil, from his people. As Pastor Bonhoeffer learned, you cannot get at evil in the world. I've written about his moral dilemma when he joined the plot to assassinate Hitler. Evil has become a product of manufacture, it is built into our whole industrial and political system, it is being manufactured every day, it is rolling off the assembly lines, it is being sold in the stores, it pollutes the air. And it's not a person!

Perhaps the way to cope with the adversary is to confront him in ourselves. We have to fight for our little bit of health. We have to make our living and dying important again. And the living and dying of others. Isn't that what poetry is about?

SEEDCORN AND WINDFALL

"We are always beginning again to live."
— Montaigne

Anyone who forsakes the child he was is already too old for po-
etry.

∽

What fascinates me about the logic of the imagination is how
unpredictable it is in practice, how full of surprises: Blake's "crooked
road," not the straight road of science and philosophy.

∽

I like to think that it is the poet's love of particulars, the things
of this world, that leads him to universals.

∽

As modernists — aren't we all? — we are inclined to believe that
the new age creates new forms. In reality, the sense of form is in-
herent in the race, substantially the same over the whole span of
recorded history. Our artistic inventions, from age to age, are es-
sentially modifications of old forms or new applications of them.
In sum, form is a constant in art, as opposed to techniques and
materials, which are variables.

∽

A badly made thing falls apart. It takes only a few years for most
of the energy to leak out of a defective work of art. To put it sim-
ply, conservation of energy is the function of form.

[119]

What makes form adventurous is its unpredictable appetite for particulars. The truly creative mind is always ready for the operations of chance. It wants to sweep into the constellation of the artwork as much as it can of the loose, floating matter that it encounters. How much accident can the work incorporate? How much of the unconscious life can the mind dredge up from its depths?

∽

The poets of any culture inherit a common tradition, by which they are sustained and replenished. What makes them separate and distinctive is the use they make of their own past, which cannot be the same as anybody else's. The difference of memories is the difference of souls.

∽

Once Theodore Roethke, in a heated defence of the melodic line that was his instrument of choice, accused Robert Lowell to his face of having "a tin ear." Cal tried to dismiss the incident as a piece of drunken foolery, but I know the charge rankled, for he recalled it to me years after Ted had died. Poets sometimes forget their poems, but never the bad things said about them.

∽

My dismay at the clutter on my desk is offset by my zest for the hunt among my papers. At an age when I should be putting my house in order, I keep accumulating bits of information, not for any particular reason and in spite of the absurdity, because I was born curious and don't know how to stop.

∽

We have all been expelled from the Garden, but the ones who suffer most in exile are those who are still permitted to dream of perfection.

∞

"Words, above everything else, are in poetry, sounds," said Wallace Stevens. Even when we read a poem silently, we tend to read it differently from prose, paying more attention to its rhythm and pitch and pace, its interplay of vowels and consonants, its line-by-line progression of subtle harmonies and discords corresponding with variable states of feeling or the flow of the mind itself. It is unfortunate that the word *texture,* in critical terminology, is commonly employed as if it defined nothing more than a surface phenomenon rather than an intrinsic property of the medium.

> But as I rav'd and grew more fierce and wilde
>   At every word,
> Methought I heard one calling, *Child!*
> And I reply'd, *My Lord.*

Those noble lines — resolving, absolving — take me back, through a chain of associations, to my undergraduate days at Harvard, where I came upon them and was shaken by them, as I still am. Simultaneously they evoke the image of a young man with clear blue eyes and a lean, sensitive countenance. This was Robert Oppenheimer, my neighbor on Mount Auburn Street. I thought of him then as being much more worldly and self-assured than I, with a physical grace and shining intelligence that made him stand out among his classmates, as did his taste for literature and the fine arts. How could one have predicted that this elegant youth, with so much civilization in him, was destined to occupy the center of the world's stage as "father of the atom bomb"? Freeman Dyson has written that Oppenheimer played the part of Prince Hamlet in the high drama of Los Alamos. Certainly, the story of his rise and fall has a tragic dimension. It is a story of genius and fame and power and conscience and intrigue and betrayal and ultimately of public humiliation and disgrace, till a malignancy of the throat finished him at sixty-two. "The physicists have known sin," he had confessed, "and this is a knowledge which they cannot lose." In a way, his lifelong attachment to the humanities served to separate him from his more single-minded colleagues in the wartime nuclear industry. He never lost his love for poetry, and no poem meant more to him than George Herbert's "The Collar," that passionate outcry of a man in spiritual doubt and torment. What chafed Herbert in his country parsonage was, emblematically, the clerical collar. Oppenheimer's collar was that of the modern scientist in bondage to the state and in the service of death — an unholy alliance.

∽

Some artists, observed Juan Gris, "are like weavers who think they can produce a material with only one set of threads and forget that there has to be another set to hold them together." The odds are that at first, in the apprentice years, one has only a single set of threads to work with, just as one has, at that early stage, only a single Time, the present, to live in, and a single self to occupy one's thoughts. A poet without a history is not precluded from composing ingenious or melodious verses, but the achievement of a mature art is dependent on accumulations of information, associated with exercises of the spirit that imbue language with a quality of innerness, a richness of psychic texture.

∽

In his book of essays, Robert Hass included an explication of one of my poems that differed radically from almost everything I thought I knew about its origin, circumstance, and meaning. Nevertheless, I felt no inclination to quarrel with his commentary. What he proposed was such a sensible and coherent interpretation of the text, consistent with the evidence available to him, that I was persuaded to accept his reading of the poem as being at least as valid as my own, even though most of his assumptions were demonstrably false.

∽

No one gave better practical advice to young writers than Chekhov. He was particularly hard on examples of stylistic inflation, such effusions as "the setting sun, bathing in the waves of the darkening sea, poured its purple gold, etc." Brevity, relevance, and specification were his criteria of excellence. A passage in one of his letters reads: "In descriptions of nature you should seize upon the little particulars, grouping them in such a way that they make a clear picture, even for eyes that are closed. For instance, you can convey the full effect of a moonlit night if you write that on the mill-dam a little glowing star-point flashed from the neck of a broken bottle. . . ."

An entry in Chekhov's notebook, dated several years later, reveals how faithful he was to his own instructions: "A bedroom. The light of the moon shines so brightly through the window that even the buttons on his nightshirt are visible."

∽

Never before, in this or any other country, have so many apprentice writers had the opportunity to study with their predecessors and ancestors. That is one explanation of why it is so difficult to detect and define a generational style in the work of our contemporaries. Instead we have an interfusion and amalgam of styles and influences, a direct transmission belt overleaping the age barrier, a two-way learning process culminating in the paradox of the young writing old, and the old writing young. Only journalists and cabalists continue to fight the war between "the ancients" and "the moderns."

∽

Two infallible touchstones of the poetic art: transformation and transcendence.

∽

Poetry is ultimately mythology, the telling of the stories of the soul. The old myths, the old gods, the old heroes have never died. They are only sleeping at the bottom of our minds, waiting for our call. We have need of them, never more desperately than now, for in their sum they epitomize the wisdom and experience of the race. At every true act of the imagination, whether in art or science, they stir fitfully. And the corollary is equally true: art and science cannot exist without myths and symbols.

∽

A major crisis in the history of poetry occurred in the last century when the novel displaced the poem as the accepted medium for story-telling. One can argue that poetry gained something in exchange, gained a good deal, by moving inward, gradually forging a link with the new science of psychoanalysis, but it seems fairly evident that in the process of cultivating this art of introversion, poets managed to lose most of their audience. A poetry deprived of narrative is also in danger of cutting itself off from its mythological roots. This dilemma will not be solved by settling for an anecdotal art, which is a species of trivialization, or by attempting to return to straight-line, sequential narration, which offers minimal aesthetic satisfactions to the modern mind. Henry James experienced a comparable difficulty in the course of his arduous enterprise and had a revelation, which he reported in prose that seems to stutter with excitement: "I realise — none too soon — that the *scenic* method is my absolute, my imperative, my *only* salvation. *The march of an action* is the thing for me to, more and more, attach myself to. . . ."

∽

Much of what passes for "meditative" poetry today suffers from the poverty of what it is meditating on.

∽

Malraux said it takes sixty years to make a man, and then he is only fit to die.

∽

Even on his deathbed, Samuel Johnson stayed true to his character and did not deviate from the Johnsonian style. When a friend offered to plump up his pillow, he summoned up the strength to reply, "No, it is doing all that a pillow can do."

࿇

When the Tzartkover Rabbi, celebrated in Hasidic lore, was asked his reason for failing to preach Torah for a long time, he gave as his answer: "There are seventy ways of reciting Torah. One of them is through silence."

࿇

Thoreau walked the long strand of Cape Cod "to see that seashore where man's works are wrecks; to put up at the true Atlantic House, where ocean is land-lord as well as sea-lord . . . where the crumbling land is the only invalid." To this day, at Race Point, the incoming breakers articulate their might with an incremental roar that changes pitch at the changing of the tides.

࿇

Be prepared for everything — even spontaneity.

࿇

In his enchanting autobiography, Konstantin Paustovsky tells the story of Bagrov, a young student revolutionary during the reign of Nicholas II, who shot Minister Stolypin dead at the Kiev opera and was sentenced to be hanged. He accepted his fate with equanimity: "What possible difference can it make to me if I eat two thousand fewer meatballs in my life?"

࿇

Paustovsky's comment on the early days of the Bolshevik Revolution: "Events took place so quickly that you missed half of them by sleeping." That is the way I've always felt, even without the excuse of a revolution, and why I insist on staying awake each night until I fall apart.

Sometimes I feel ashamed that I've written so few poems on political themes, on the causes that agitate me. But then I remind myself that to be a poet at all in twentieth-century America is to commit a political act.

Of all modern institutions the State, which is the political arm of the economy, is the most terrifying, the most monstrous instrument of power. All societies profess that they are organized for the sake of human welfare and freedom, but in practice power becomes an end in itself, a self-perpetuating coalition of egos, supported by bureaucracies that gradually suffocate the spirit of a people. "Society everywhere," wrote Emerson presciently, "is in conspiracy against the manhood of every one of its members. . . . The virtue in most request is conformity. Self-reliance is its aversion."

Throughout the course of history politicians have had reason to fear the wicked tongue of poets, but poets, at least in this country, do not fear politicians — they simply distrust anybody who makes a vocation out of the pursuit of power. They tend to agree with old John Adams that "Power always thinks it has a great soul and vast views beyond the comprehension of the weak and that it is doing God's service when it is violating all His laws."

Poets by nature are predisposed to think of single-mindedness, any kind of fanaticism, as a curse. The spirit of poetry renounces the Shah of Iran no more and no less than it renounces the righteous ayatollahs.

In his eighty-seventh year, Miró told an interviewer that he felt closest to "the young — all the young generations." From childhood to age, he ruminated, "I have always lived a very intense life, almost like a monk, an austere life. It comes out in little leaves, floating about, dispersing themselves. But the trunk of the tree and the branches remain solid."

Yes, he admitted, his style had changed — changed several times, in fact, during his long life. But these changes did not imply a rejection of what he had done before. Looking back, he could see a continuity in the essence of his work, which is nourished at every stage "by all of my past, the great human past. And what looks like a zig-zag is really a straight line."

∽

Years ago I came to the realization that the most poignant of all lyric tensions stems from the awareness that we are dying every moment we live. To embrace such knowledge and yet to remain compassionate and whole — that is the consummation of the endeavor of art.

∽

The first grand concept I had was of death, my death, everyone's death. Through the circumstances of my childhood it was the fox at my breast, wrapped under my coat, a consuming terror. I could not sleep at night, thinking about dying. And then I realized that if I wanted to retain my sanity I had to learn how to live with this dreadful knowledge, transforming it into a principle of creation instead of destruction. The first step toward salvation was the recognition of the narrowness of my world of sympathies. My affections had to flow outward and circulate through the natural order of things. Only then did I understand that, in the great chain of being, death as well as life has its own beauty and magnificence.

ACKNOWLEDGMENTS

The poems and other contents of this volume originally appeared, not always in exactly the same form, in the following publications, to whose editors grateful acknowledgment is made:

The American Poetry Review
    The Tumbling of Worms
    The Round
    Passing Through
    At the Tomb of Walt Whitman

Antaeus
    The Snakes of September
    The Scene
    Three Small Parables for My Poet Friends
    Seedcorn and Windfall

The Atlantic
    The Abduction
    The Image-Maker
    The Wellfleet Whale

The New Yorker
    Raccoon Journal

Salmagundi
    Lamplighter: 1914
    The Long Boat

"From Feathers to Iron" originated as a lecture delivered at the Library of Congress during my tenure as Consultant in Poetry and was subsequently published by the Library in pamphlet form.

"Robert Lowell: The Sense of a Life" is based on an article that first appeared in the *New York Times Book Review* and on my editorial introduction to a recorded album of Lowell's readings, issued by the Library of Congress. The excerpt quoted from one of Lowell's letters to me is copyrighted by the estate of Robert Lowell and is used with permission.

"At the Tomb of Walt Whitman" is adapted from a talk given at the Pierpont Morgan Library in New York on March 15, 1984, in celebration of the fiftieth anniversary of the Academy of American Poets.

"The Wisdom of the Body" is based on a commencement address given at Sarah Lawrence College and first published, in different form, by *Antaeus* under the title "The Life of Poetry."

"The Layers: Some Notes on 'The Abduction' " was written for *Singular Voices,* edited by Stephen Berg and published by Avon Books. A version of this essay appeared in *Ironwood.*

"Table Talk" is a somewhat abbreviated version of a *Paris Review* interview, reprinted here with permission of Chris Busa and *Paris Review.*

"The Wellfleet Whale" was first read at Harvard College in 1981 as the Phi Beta Kappa Poem. "Day of Foreboding," "The Snakes of September," and "The Wellfleet Whale" have appeared in a chapbook, *The Wellfleet Whale and Companion Poems,* published by Sheep Meadow Press.

"The Abduction" and "The Wellfleet Whale" have been reprinted in *Contemporary American Poetry,* fourth edition, edited by A. Poulin, Jr., and published by Houghton Mifflin.

The lines chosen for the epigraph of this book are from my poem "Around Pastor Bonhoeffer," first published in *The Testing-Tree* and subsequently in *The Poems of Stanley Kunitz: 1928–1978.*

I wish to express my special gratitude to the National Endowment for the Arts for awarding me a Senior Fellowship during my preparation of this book.